MznLnx

Missing Links Exam Preps

Exam Prep for

Beginning and Intermediate Algebra

Lial & Hornsby & McGinnis, 3rd Edition

The MznLnx Exam Prep is your link from the texbook and lecture to your exams.
The MznLnx Exam Preps are unauthorized and comprehensive reviews of your textbooks.

All material provided by MznLnx and Rico Publications (c) 2010
Textbook publishers and textbook authors do not particpate in or contribute to these reviews.

MznLnx

Rico Publications

Exam Prep for Beginning and Intermediate Algebra
3rd Edition
Lial & Hornsby & McGinnis

Publisher: Raymond Houge
Assistant Editor: Michael Rouger
Text and Cover Designer: Lisa Buckner
Marketing Manager: Sara Swagger
Project Manager, Editorial Production: Jerry Emerson
Art Director: Vernon Lowerui

Product Manager: Dave Mason
Editorial Assitant: Rachel Guzmanji
Pedagogy: Debra Long
Cover Image: Jim Reed/Getty Images
Text and Cover Printer: City Printing, Inc.
Compositor: Media Mix, Inc.

(c) 2010 Rico Publications

ALL RIGHTS RESERVED. No part of this work covered by the copyright may be reproduced or used in any form or by an means--graphic, electronic, or mechanical, including photocopying, recording, taping, Web distribution, information storage, and retrieval systems, or in any other manner--without the written permission of the publisher.

For more information about our products, contact us at:
Dave.Mason@RicoPublications.com

For permission to use material from this text or product, submit a request online to:
Dave.Mason@RicoPublications.com

Printed in the United States
ISBN:

Contents

CHAPTER 1
The Real Number System — 1

CHAPTER 2
Linear Equations and Inequalities in One Variable; Applications — 10

CHAPTER 3
Linear Equations in Two Variables — 16

CHAPTER 4
Exponents and Polynomials — 19

CHAPTER 5
Factoring and Applications — 26

CHAPTER 6
Rational Expressions and Applications — 31

CHAPTER 7
Equations of Lines; Functions — 34

CHAPTER 8
Systems of Linear Equations — 39

CHAPTER 9
Inequalities and Absolute Value — 44

CHAPTER 10
Roots, Radicals, and Root Functions — 47

CHAPTER 11
Quadratic Equations, Inequalities, and Functions — 57

CHAPTER 12
Inverse, Exponential, and Logarithmic Functions — 63

CHAPTER 13
Nonlinear Functions, Conic Sections, and Nonlinear Systems — 65

CHAPTER 14
Sequences and Series — 69

ANSWER KEY — 81

TO THE STUDENT

COMPREHENSIVE

The *MznLnx* Exam Prep series is designed to help you pass your exams. Editors at MznLnx review your textbooks and then prepare these practice exams to help you master the textbook material. Unlike study guides, workbooks, and practice tests provided by the texbook publisher and textbook authors, *MznLnx* gives you **all** of the material in each chapter in exam form, not just samples, so you can be sure to nail your exam.

MECHANICAL

The MznLnx Exam Prep series creates exams that will help you learn the subject matter as well as test you on your understanding. Each question is designed to help you master the concept. Just working through the exams, you gain an understanding of the subject--its a simple mechanical process that produces success.

INTEGRATED STUDY GUIDE AND REVIEW

MznLnx is not just a set of exams designed to test you, its also a comprehensive review of the subject content. Each exam question is also a review of the concept, making sure that you will get the answer correct without having to go to other sources of material. You learn as you go! Its the easiest way to pass an exam.

HUMOR

Studying can be tedious and dry. MznLnx's instructional design includes moderate humor within the exam questions on occassion, to break the tedium and revitalize the brain

Chapter 1. The Real Number System

1. In mathematics, the _____ of a real number is its numerical value without regard to its sign. So, for example, 3 is the _____ of both 3 and −3.

   The _____ of a number a is denoted by $|a|$.

   a. AKS primality test
   b. Abelian P-root group
   c. ADE classification
   d. Absolute value

2. In its simplest meaning in mathematics and logic, an _____ is an action or procedure which produces a new value from one or more input values. There are two common types of operations: unary and binary. Unary operations involve only one value, such as negation and trigonometric functions.
   a. AKS primality test
   b. Abelian P-root group
   c. ADE classification
   d. Operation

3. In mathematics, especially in elementary arithmetic, _____ is an arithmetic operation which is the inverse of multiplication.

   Specifically, if c times b equals a, written:

   $$c \times b = a$$

   where b is not zero, then a divided by b equals c, written:

   $$\frac{a}{b} = c$$

   For instance,

   $$\frac{6}{3} = 2$$

   since

   $$2 \times 3 = 6.$$

   In the above expression, a is called the dividend, b the divisor and c the quotient.

a. 2-bridge knot
b. -module
c. -equivalence
d. Division

4. In mathematics, the complex numbers are an extension of the real numbers obtained by adjoining an imaginary unit, denoted i, which satisfies:

$$i^2 = -1.$$

Every _____ can be written in the form a + bi, where a and b are real numbers called the real part and the imaginary part of the _____, respectively.

Complex numbers are a field, and thus have addition, subtraction, multiplication, and division operations. These operations extend the corresponding operations on real numbers, although with a number of additional elegant and useful properties, e.g., negative real numbers can be obtained by squaring complex (imaginary) numbers.

a. -equivalence
b. -module
c. 2-bridge knot
d. Complex number

5. _____ is the mathematical process of putting things together. The plus sign '+' means that numbers are added together. For example, in the picture on the right, there are 3 + 2 apples--meaning three apples and two other apples--which is the same as five apples, since 3 + 2 = 5.
a. ADE classification
b. AKS primality test
c. Abelian P-root group
d. Addition

6. _____ is one of the four basic arithmetic operations; it is the inverse of addition, meaning that if we start with any number and add any number and then subtract the same number we added, we return to the number we started with. _____ is denoted by a minus sign in infix notation.

The traditional names for the parts of the formula

c − b = a

are minuend (c) − subtrahend (b) = difference (a.)

Chapter 1. The Real Number System

   a. Subtraction
   b. -equivalence
   c. -module
   d. 2-bridge knot

7. A _____ is a three-dimensional solid object bounded by six square faces, facets or sides, with three meeting at each vertex. The _____ can also be called a regular hexahedron and is one of the five Platonic solids. It is a special kind of square prism, of rectangular parallelepiped and of trigonal trapezohedron.

   a. -equivalence
   b. Cube
   c. 2-bridge knot
   d. -module

8. In mathematics, the word _____ is a term for any well-formed combination of mathematical symbols. For example,

   $x^2 + 3x - 4$

is an _____, while

   $)x) / 0$

is not, because the parentheses are not balanced and division by zero is undefined.

Being an _____ is a syntactic concept - the meaning of the variables is irrelevant, but different fields have different notions of validity.â€See formal language for how expressions are constructed, and formal semantics for meaning.

   a. Arity
   b. Orthogonal
   c. Unit ring
   d. Expression

Chapter 1. The Real Number System

9. In elementary algebra, a _____ is a polynomial with two terms--the sum of two monomials--often bound by parenthesis or brackets when operated upon. It is the simplest kind of polynomial other than monomials.

- The _____ $a^2 - b^2$ can be factored as the product of two other binomials:

    $a^2 - b^2 = (a + b)(a - b.)$

    This is a special case of the more general formula: $a^{n+1} - b^{n+1} = (a-b) \sum_{k=0}^{n} a^k b^{n-k}$.

- The product of a pair of linear binomials $(ax + b)$ and $(cx + d)$ is:

    $(ax + b)(cx + d) = acx^2 + axd + bcx + bd.$

- A _____ raised to the nth power, represented as

    $(a + b)^n$

    can be expanded by means of the _____ theorem or, equivalently, using Pascal's triangle. Taking a simple example, the perfect square _____ $(p + q)^2$ can be found by squaring the :first digit, adding twice the product of the first and second digit and finally adding the square of the second digit, to give $p^2 + 2pq + q^2$.

a. Generalized arithmetic progression
b. Theory of equations
c. Content
d. Binomial

10. In group theory, a branch of mathematics, the term _____ is used in two closely related senses:

    - the _____ of a group is its cardinality, i.e. the number of its elements;
    - the _____, sometimes period, of an element a of a group is the smallest positive integer m such that $a^m = e$ (where e denotes the identity element of the group, and a^m denotes the product of m copies of a.) If no such m exists, we say that a has infinite _____. All elements of finite groups have finite _____.

We denote the _____ of a group G by ord(G) or $|G|$ and the _____ of an element a by ord(a) or $|a|$.

Example. The symmetric group S_3 has the following multiplication table.

This group has six elements, so ord(S_3) = 6.

Chapter 1. The Real Number System

a. Order
b. Outer automorphism group
c. Artin group
d. Index calculus algorithm

11. In algebra and computer programming, when a number or expression is both preceded and followed by an operator such as minus or times, a rule is needed to specify which operator should be applied first; this rule is known as a _____, or more informally order of operation. From the earliest use of mathematical notation, multiplication took precedence over addition, whichever side of a number it appeared on. Thus 3 + 4 × 5 = 5 × 4 + 3 = 23.

a. Formal power series
b. Precedence rule
c. Setoid
d. Planar ternary ring

12. In mathematics, an _____ is a statement about the relative size or order of two objects, or about whether they are the same or not

- The notation a < b means that a is less than b.
- The notation a > b means that a is greater than b.
- The notation a ≠ b means that a is not equal to b, but does not say that one is bigger than the other or even that they can be compared in size.

In all these cases, a is not equal to b, hence, '_____'.

These relations are known as strict _____

- The notation a ≤ b means that a is less than or equal to b (or, equivalently, not greater than b);
- The notation a ≥ b means that a is greater than or equal to b (or, equivalently, not smaller than b);

An additional use of the notation is to show that one quantity is much greater than another, normally by several orders of magnitude.

- The notation a ≪ b means that a is much less than b.
- The notation a ≫ b means that a is much greater than b.

If the sense of the _____ is the same for all values of the variables for which its members are defined, then the _____ is called an 'absolute' or 'unconditional' _____. If the sense of an _____ holds only for certain values of the variables involved, but is reversed or destroyed for other values of the variables, it is called a conditional _____.

One can apply the same algebraic operations to inequalities as one would apply for solving equalities. For example, to find x for the _____ 10x > 20 one would divide 20 by 10 to obtain x > 2.

a. Inequality
b. ADE classification
c. AKS primality test
d. Abelian P-root group

13. A _____ is a symbol that stands for a value that may vary; the term usually occurs in opposition to constant, which is a symbol for a non-varying value, i.e. completely fixed or fixed in the context of use. The concepts of constants and variables are fundamental to all modern mathematics, science, engineering, and computer programming.

Much of the basic theory for which we use variables today, such as school geometry and algebra, was developed thousands of years ago, but the use of symbolic formulae and variables is only several hundreds of years old.

a. -equivalence
b. 2-bridge knot
c. Variable
d. -module

14. In mathematics, a _____ is a rectangular array of numbers. This way, matrices can record data that depend on multiple parameters. In particular they are used to keep track of the coefficients of multiple linear equations. Matrices are closely connected to linear transformations, which are higher-dimensional analogs of linear functions, i.e., functions of the form f(x) = c Â· x, where c is a constant. This map corresponds to a _____ with one row and column, with entry c. In addition to a number of elementary, entrywise operations such as _____ addition a key notion is _____ multiplication, which displays a number of features not encountered in numbers; for example, products of matrices depend on the order of the factors, unlike products of real numbers, say, where c Â· d = d Â· c for any two numbers c and d.

a. Commutativity
b. Heap
c. Polynomial expression
d. Matrix

15. The _____ are natural numbers including 0 ' href='/wiki/0_(number)'>0, 1, 2, 3, ...) and their negatives (0, −1, −2, −3, ...). They are numbers that can be written without a fractional or decimal component, and fall within the set {...

a. Integers
b. ADE classification
c. Abelian P-root group
d. AKS primality test

16. In mathematics, the _____ of a number n is the number that, when added to n, yields zero. The _____ of F is denoted −F.

For example, the _____ of 7 is −7, because 7 + (−7) = 0, and the _____ of −0.3 is 0.3, because −0.3 + 0.3 = 0.

a. Additive inverse
b. Isomorphism class
c. Interior algebra
d. Artinian ideal

17. In geometry, a _____ is a straight curve. When geometry is used to model the real world, lines are used to represent straight objects with negligible width and height. Lines are an idealisation of such objects and have no width or height at all and are usually considered to be infinitely long.
a. -equivalence
b. -module
c. 2-bridge knot
d. Line

18. In mathematics, a _____ is any number that can be expressed in the form

$$\frac{a}{b}, a, b \in \mathbb{Z}, b \neq 0$$

which says 'a divided by b, given that a and b are integers and b does not equal zero'. Since the denominator b may be equal to 1, every integer is a _____. The set of all rational numbers is denoted $\mathbb{Q}$ (for quotient.)

a. Number system
b. Ratio
c. Rational number
d. -equivalence

Chapter 1. The Real Number System

19. In mathematics, a _____ is a polynomial equation of the second degree. The general form is

$$ax^2 + bx + c = 0$$

The quadratic coefficient a is the coefficient of x^2, the linear coefficient b is the coefficient of x, and c is the constant coefficient, also called the free term or constant term.

Quadratic equations are called quadratic because the variable in the leading term is squared.

  a. Cubic function
  b. Rationalisation
  c. Quadratic equation
  d. Difference of two squares

20. The _____ of a Lie algebra $\mathfrak{g}$ is a particular ideal of $\mathfrak{g}$.

Let $\mathfrak{g}$ be a Lie algebra. The _____ of $\mathfrak{g}$ is defined as the largest solvable ideal of $\mathfrak{g}$.

  a. Class sum
  b. Cyclically reduced word
  c. Radical
  d. Garside element

21. In mathematics, an _____ is the finite or bounded case of a conic section, the geometric shape that results from cutting a circular conical or cylindrical surface with an oblique plane . It is also the locus of all points of the plane whose distances to two fixed points add to the same constant.

Ellipses also arise as images of a circle or a sphere under parallel projection, and some cases of perspective projection.

  a. ADE classification
  b. Abelian P-root group
  c. Ellipse
  d. AKS primality test

22. In mathematics, a _____ or reciprocal for a number x, denoted by $1/x$ or x^{-1}, is a number which when multiplied by x yields the multiplicative identity, 1. The _____ of x is also called the reciprocal of x. The _____ of a fraction a/b is b/a.

a. 2-bridge knot
b. Multiplicative inverse
c. -equivalence
d. -module

23. In mathematics the _____ of a set which is equipped with the operation of addition is an element which, when added to any element x in the set, yields x. One of the most familiar additive identities is the number 0 from elementary mathematics, but additive identities occur in other mathematical structures where addition is defined, such as in groups and rings.

- The _____ familiar from elementary mathematics is zero, denoted 0. For example,

  5 + 0 = 5 = 0 + 5.

- In the natural numbers N and all of its supersets (the integers Z, the rational numbers Q, the real numbers R, or the complex numbers C), the _____ is 0. Thus for any one of these numbers n,

  n + 0 = n = 0 + n.

Let N be a set which is closed under the operation of addition, denoted +. An _____ for N is any element e such that for any element n in N,

  e + n = n = n + e.

a. External
b. Universal algebra
c. Identity element
d. Additive identity

24. In mathematics, an _____ is a special type of element of a set with respect to a binary operation on that set. It leaves other elements unchanged when combined with them. This is used for groups and related concepts.
a. Identity element
b. Orthogonal
c. Algebraic K-theory
d. Isomorphism class

Chapter 2. Linear Equations and Inequalities in One Variable; Applications

1. In mathematics, a _____ is a constant multiplicative factor of a certain object. For example, in the expression $9x^2$, the _____ of x^2 is 9.

The object can be such things as a variable, a vector, a function, etc.

   a. Tschirnhaus transformation
   b. Constant term
   c. Vandermonde polynomial
   d. Coefficient

2. A _____ is a symbol that stands for a value that may vary; the term usually occurs in opposition to constant, which is a symbol for a non-varying value, i.e. completely fixed or fixed in the context of use. The concepts of constants and variables are fundamental to all modern mathematics, science, engineering, and computer programming.

Much of the basic theory for which we use variables today, such as school geometry and algebra, was developed thousands of years ago, but the use of symbolic formulae and variables is only several hundreds of years old.

   a. 2-bridge knot
   b. Variable
   c. -equivalence
   d. -module

3. In mathematics, and more specifically set theory, the _____ is the unique set having no (zero) members. Some axiomatic set theories assure that the _____ exists by including an axiom of _____; in other theories, its existence can be deduced. Many possible properties of sets are trivially true for the _____.
   a. Abelian P-root group
   b. AKS primality test
   c. ADE classification
   d. Empty set

4. _____ is the mathematical process of putting things together. The plus sign '+' means that numbers are added together. For example, in the picture on the right, there are 3 + 2 apples--meaning three apples and two other apples--which is the same as five apples, since 3 + 2 = 5.
   a. Addition
   b. AKS primality test
   c. ADE classification
   d. Abelian P-root group

5. In mathematics, the word _____ is a term for any well-formed combination of mathematical symbols. For example,

$$x^2 + 3x - 4$$

is an _____, while

$$)x) / 0$$

is not, because the parentheses are not balanced and division by zero is undefined.

Being an _____ is a syntactic concept - the meaning of the variables is irrelevant, but different fields have different notions of validity.â€¢See formal language for how expressions are constructed, and formal semantics for meaning.

   a. Unit ring
   b. Orthogonal
   c. Expression
   d. Arity

6. In geometry and trigonometry, an _____ is the figure formed by two rays sharing a common endpoint, called the vertex of the _____ . The magnitude of the _____ is the 'amount of rotation' that separates the two rays, and can be measured by considering the length of circular arc swept out when one ray is rotated about the vertex to coincide with the other Where there is no possibility of confusion, the term '_____' is used interchangeably for both the geometric configuration itself and for its angular magnitude (which is simply a numerical quantity.)
   a. AKS primality test
   b. ADE classification
   c. Abelian P-root group
   d. Angle

7. In mathematics, there are several meanings of _____ depending on the subject.

A _____, usually denoted by ° (the _____ symbol), is a measurement of plane angle, representing $\frac{1}{360}$ of a full rotation. When that angle is with respect to a reference meridian, it indicates a location along a great circle of a sphere, such as Earth , Mars, or the celestial sphere.

   a. Degree
   b. Relation algebra
   c. Symmetric difference
   d. Median algebra

Chapter 2. Linear Equations and Inequalities in One Variable; Applications

8. The _____ are natural numbers including 0 ' href='/wiki/0_(number)'>0, 1, 2, 3, ...) and their negatives (0, −1, −2, −3, ...). They are numbers that can be written without a fractional or decimal component, and fall within the set {...
   a. AKS primality test
   b. ADE classification
   c. Abelian P-root group
   d. Integers

9. A _____ is perfectly round geometrical object in three-dimensional space, such as the shape of a round ball. Like a circle in two dimensions, a perfect _____ is completely symmetrical around its center, with all points on the surface lying the same distance r from the center point. This distance r is known as the radius of the _____.
   a. Generalized flag variety
   b. Stable normal bundle
   c. Sphere
   d. Grassmannian

10. A _____ is an expression which compares quantities relative to each other. The most common examples involve two quantities, but in theory any number of quantities can be compared. In mathematical terms, they are represented by separating each quantity with a colon, for example the _____ 2:3, which is read as the _____ 'two to three'.
    a. Ratio
    b. Number system
    c. -equivalence
    d. Rational number

11. In mathematics, a _____ in a (unital) ring R is an invertible element of R, i.e. an element u such that there is a v in R with

   $uv = vu = 1_R$, where 1_R is the multiplicative identity element.

That is, u is an invertible element of the multiplicative monoid of R. If $0 \neq 1$ in the ring, then 0 is not a _____.

Unfortunately, the term _____ is also used to refer to the identity element 1_R of the ring, in expressions like ring with a _____ or _____ ring, and also e.g. '_____' matrix.

a. Ascending chain condition on principal ideals
b. Ore condition
c. Unit
d. Ore extension

12. In linear algebra, two n-by-n matrices A and B are called _____ if

$$B = P^{-1}AP$$

for some invertible n-by-n matrix P. _____ matrices represent the same linear transformation under two different bases, with P being the change of basis matrix.

The matrix P is sometimes called a similarity transformation. In the context of matrix groups, similarity is sometimes referred to as conjugacy, with _____ matrices being conjugate.

a. Zero matrix
b. Skew-symmetric
c. Cartan matrix
d. Similar

13. A _____ is one of the basic shapes of geometry: a polygon with three corners or vertices and three sides or edges which are line segments. A _____ with vertices A, B, and C is denoted ABC.

In Euclidean geometry any three non-collinear points determine a unique _____ and a unique plane (i.e. a two-dimensional Euclidean space.)

a. 2-bridge knot
b. -module
c. -equivalence
d. Triangle

Chapter 2. Linear Equations and Inequalities in One Variable; Applications

14. In mathematics, the term _____ is used to describe an algebraic structures which in some sense cannot be divided by a smaller structure of the same type. Put another way, an algebraic structure is _____ if the kernel of every homomorphism is either the whole structure or a single element. Some examples are:

- A group is called a _____ group if it does not contain a non-trivial proper normal subgroup.
- A ring is called a _____ ring if it does not contain a non-trivial two sided ideal.
- A module is called a _____ module if does not contain a non-trivial submodule.
- An algebra is called a _____ algebra if does not contain a non-trivial two sided ideal.

The general pattern is that the structure admits no non-trivial congruence relations.

a. Commutativity
b. Polarization identity
c. Linear combinations
d. Simple

15. In mathematics, an _____ is a statement about the relative size or order of two objects, or about whether they are the same or not

- The notation $a < b$ means that a is less than b.
- The notation $a > b$ means that a is greater than b.
- The notation $a \neq b$ means that a is not equal to b, but does not say that one is bigger than the other or even that they can be compared in size.

In all these cases, a is not equal to b, hence, '_____'.

These relations are known as strict _____

- The notation $a \leq b$ means that a is less than or equal to b (or, equivalently, not greater than b);
- The notation $a \geq b$ means that a is greater than or equal to b (or, equivalently, not smaller than b);

An additional use of the notation is to show that one quantity is much greater than another, normally by several orders of magnitude.

- The notation $a \ll b$ means that a is much less than b.
- The notation $a \gg b$ means that a is much greater than b.

If the sense of the _____ is the same for all values of the variables for which its members are defined, then the _____ is called an 'absolute' or 'unconditional' _____. If the sense of an _____ holds only for certain values of the variables involved, but is reversed or destroyed for other values of the variables, it is called a conditional _____.

One can apply the same algebraic operations to inequalities as one would apply for solving equalities. For example, to find x for the _____ 10x > 20 one would divide 20 by 10 to obtain x > 2.

a. ADE classification
b. Inequality
c. Abelian P-root group
d. AKS primality test

16. In mathematics a _____ is an inequality which involves a linear function.

When operating in terms of real numbers, linear inequalities are the ones written in the forms

$$f(x) < b \text{ or } f(x) \leq b,$$

where f(x) is a linear functional in real numbers and b is a constant real number. Alternatively, these may be viewed as

$$g(x) < 0 \text{ or } g(x) \leq 0,$$

where g(x) is an affine function.

a. Fundamental theorem of linear algebra
b. Semi-simple operators
c. Flag
d. Linear inequality

Chapter 3. Linear Equations in Two Variables

1. In geometry, a _____ is a straight curve. When geometry is used to model the real world, lines are used to represent straight objects with negligible width and height. Lines are an idealisation of such objects and have no width or height at all and are usually considered to be infinitely long.
    a. -module
    b. -equivalence
    c. 2-bridge knot
    d. Line

2. A _____ is a symbol that stands for a value that may vary; the term usually occurs in opposition to constant, which is a symbol for a non-varying value, i.e. completely fixed or fixed in the context of use. The concepts of constants and variables are fundamental to all modern mathematics, science, engineering, and computer programming.

    Much of the basic theory for which we use variables today, such as school geometry and algebra, was developed thousands of years ago, but the use of symbolic formulae and variables is only several hundreds of years old.

    a. -equivalence
    b. Variable
    c. 2-bridge knot
    d. -module

3. In mathematics, a (B, N) _____ is a structure on groups of Lie type that allows one to give uniform proofs of many results, instead of giving a large number of case-by-case proofs. Roughly speaking, it shows that all such groups are similar to the general linear group over a field. They were invented by the mathematician Jacques Tits, and are also sometimes known as Tits systems.
    a. Group representations
    b. Rank of a group
    c. Pair
    d. Group action

4. In mathematics, a _____ is a collection of linear equations involving the same set of variables. For example,

$$3x + 2y - z = 1$$
$$2x - 2y + 4z = -2$$
$$-x + \tfrac{1}{2}y - z = 0$$

is a system of three equations in the three variables x, y, z. A solution to a linear system is an assignment of numbers to the variables such that all the equations are simultaneously satisfied.

a. -module
b. -equivalence
c. Simultaneous equations
d. System of linear equations

5. In mathematics, a _____ is a flat surface. Planes can arise as subspaces of some higher dimensional space, as with the walls of a room, or they may enjoy an independent existence in their own right, as in the setting of Euclidean geometry
   a. -equivalence
   b. Similarity
   c. Plane
   d. -module

6. In mathematics, a _____ is a polynomial equation of the second degree. The general form is

$$ax^2 + bx + c = 0$$

The quadratic coefficient a is the coefficient of x^2, the linear coefficient b is the coefficient of x, and c is the constant coefficient, also called the free term or constant term.

Quadratic equations are called quadratic because the variable in the leading term is squared.

   a. Difference of two squares
   b. Cubic function
   c. Rationalisation
   d. Quadratic equation

7. In mathematics, the term _____ is used to describe an algebraic structures which in some sense cannot be divided by a smaller structure of the same type. Put another way, an algebraic structure is _____ if the kernel of every homomorphism is either the whole structure or a single element. Some examples are:

   - A group is called a _____ group if it does not contain a non-trivial proper normal subgroup.
   - A ring is called a _____ ring if it does not contain a non-trivial two sided ideal.
   - A module is called a _____ module if does not contain a non-trivial submodule.
   - An algebra is called a _____ algebra if does not contain a non-trivial two sided ideal.

The general pattern is that the structure admits no non-trivial congruence relations.

Chapter 3. Linear Equations in Two Variables

a. Linear combinations
b. Simple
c. Commutativity
d. Polarization identity

8. In geometry, two lines or planes (or a line and a plane), are considered _____ to each other if they form congruent adjacent angles (an L-shape.) The term may be used as a noun or adjective. Thus, referring to Figure 1, the line AB is the _____ to CD through the point B. Note that by definition, a line is infinitely long, and strictly speaking AB and CD in this example represent line segments of two infinitely long lines.
   a. -equivalence
   b. -module
   c. 2-bridge knot
   d. Perpendicular

9. In mathematics, the complex numbers are an extension of the real numbers obtained by adjoining an imaginary unit, denoted i, which satisfies:

$$i^2 = -1.$$

Every _____ can be written in the form a + bi, where a and b are real numbers called the real part and the imaginary part of the _____, respectively.

Complex numbers are a field, and thus have addition, subtraction, multiplication, and division operations. These operations extend the corresponding operations on real numbers, although with a number of additional elegant and useful properties, e.g., negative real numbers can be obtained by squaring complex (imaginary) numbers.

   a. -module
   b. -equivalence
   c. 2-bridge knot
   d. Complex number

Chapter 4. Exponents and Polynomials

1. In mathematics, the word _____ is a term for any well-formed combination of mathematical symbols. For example,

    $x^2 + 3x - 4$

is an _____, while

)x) / 0

is not, because the parentheses are not balanced and division by zero is undefined.

Being an _____ is a syntactic concept - the meaning of the variables is irrelevant, but different fields have different notions of validity.â€See formal language for how expressions are constructed, and formal semantics for meaning.

   a. Arity
   b. Orthogonal
   c. Unit ring
   d. Expression

2. The _____ are natural numbers including 0 ' href='/wiki/0_(number)'>0, 1, 2, 3, ...) and their negatives (0, −1, −2, −3, ...). They are numbers that can be written without a fractional or decimal component, and fall within the set {...
   a. AKS primality test
   b. ADE classification
   c. Abelian P-root group
   d. Integers

3. _____ is the mathematical process of putting things together. The plus sign '+' means that numbers are added together. For example, in the picture on the right, there are 3 + 2 apples--meaning three apples and two other apples--which is the same as five apples, since 3 + 2 = 5.
   a. AKS primality test
   b. ADE classification
   c. Addition
   d. Abelian P-root group

4. A _____ is a symbol that stands for a value that may vary; the term usually occurs in opposition to constant, which is a symbol for a non-varying value, i.e. completely fixed or fixed in the context of use. The concepts of constants and variables are fundamental to all modern mathematics, science, engineering, and computer programming.

Much of the basic theory for which we use variables today, such as school geometry and algebra, was developed thousands of years ago, but the use of symbolic formulae and variables is only several hundreds of years old.

Chapter 4. Exponents and Polynomials

   a. Variable
   b. -equivalence
   c. 2-bridge knot
   d. -module

5. In mathematics, a _____ is a constant multiplicative factor of a certain object. For example, in the expression $9x^2$, the _____ of x^2 is 9.

The object can be such things as a variable, a vector, a function, etc.

   a. Tschirnhaus transformation
   b. Constant term
   c. Vandermonde polynomial
   d. Coefficient

6. In mathematics, there are several meanings of _____ depending on the subject.

A _____, usually denoted by ° (the _____ symbol), is a measurement of plane angle, representing $1/360$ of a full rotation. When that angle is with respect to a reference meridian, it indicates a location along a great circle of a sphere, such as Earth, Mars, or the celestial sphere.

   a. Symmetric difference
   b. Median algebra
   c. Relation algebra
   d. Degree

7. In elementary algebra, a _____ is a polynomial consisting of three terms; in other words, a _____ is the sum of three monomials. It can be factored using simple steps.

In linguistics, a _____ is a fixed expression which is made from three words; e.g. 'lights, camera, action', 'signed, sealed, delivered'.

   a. Polynomial Diophantine equation
   b. Finitary operation
   c. Hall polynomials
   d. Trinomial

Chapter 4. Exponents and Polynomials

8. In elementary algebra, a _____ is a polynomial with two terms--the sum of two monomials--often bound by parenthesis or brackets when operated upon. It is the simplest kind of polynomial other than monomials.

- The _____ $a^2 - b^2$ can be factored as the product of two other binomials:

    $a^2 - b^2 = (a + b)(a - b.)$

    This is a special case of the more general formula:

    $$a^{n+1} - b^{n+1} = (a - b) \sum_{k=0}^{n} a^k b^{n-k}.$$

- The product of a pair of linear binomials (ax + b) and (cx + d) is:

    $(ax + b)(cx + d) = acx^2 + axd + bcx + bd.$

- A _____ raised to the nth power, represented as

    $(a + b)^n$

    can be expanded by means of the _____ theorem or, equivalently, using Pascal's triangle. Taking a simple example, the perfect square _____ $(p + q)^2$ can be found by squaring the :first digit, adding twice the product of the first and second digit and finally adding the square of the second digit, to give $p^2 + 2pq + q^2$.

a. Theory of equations
b. Generalized arithmetic progression
c. Content
d. Binomial

9. In mathematics, the word _____ means two different things in the context of polynomials:

    - The first meaning is a product of powers of variables, or formally any value obtained from 1 by finitely many multiplications by a variable. If only a single variable x is considered this means that any _____ is either 1 or a power x^n of x, with n a positive integer. If several variables are considered, say, x, y, z, then each can be given an exponent, so that any _____ is of the form $x^a y^b z^c$ with a,b,c nonnegative integers (taking note that any exponent 0 makes the corresponding factor equal to 1.)
    - The second meaning of _____ includes monomials in the first sense, but also allows multiplication by any constant, so that − $7x^5$ and $(3 − 4i)x^4 y z^{13}$ are also considered to be monomials (the second example assuming polynomials in x, y, z over the complex numbers are considered.)

With either definition, the set of monomials is a subset of all polynomials that is closed under multiplication.

Both uses of this notion can be found, and in many cases the distinction is simply ignored, see for instance examples for the first and second meaning, and an unclear definition. In informal discussions the distinction is seldom important, and tendency is towards the broader second meaning. When studying the structure of polynomials however, one often definitely needs a notion with the first meaning.

Chapter 4. Exponents and Polynomials

a. Power sum symmetric polynomial
b. Schur polynomials
c. Diagonal form
d. Monomial

10. In its simplest meaning in mathematics and logic, an _____ is an action or procedure which produces a new value from one or more input values. There are two common types of operations: unary and binary. Unary operations involve only one value, such as negation and trigonometric functions.

a. Abelian P-root group
b. ADE classification
c. AKS primality test
d. Operation

11. _____ is one of the four basic arithmetic operations; it is the inverse of addition, meaning that if we start with any number and add any number and then subtract the same number we added, we return to the number we started with. _____ is denoted by a minus sign in infix notation.

The traditional names for the parts of the formula

c − b = a

are minuend (c) − subtrahend (b) = difference (a.)

a. -module
b. -equivalence
c. 2-bridge knot
d. Subtraction

12. In mathematics, the complex numbers are an extension of the real numbers obtained by adjoining an imaginary unit, denoted i, which satisfies:

$$i^2 = -1.$$

Every _____ can be written in the form a + bi, where a and b are real numbers called the real part and the imaginary part of the _____, respectively.

Complex numbers are a field, and thus have addition, subtraction, multiplication, and division operations. These operations extend the corresponding operations on real numbers, although with a number of additional elegant and useful properties, e.g., negative real numbers can be obtained by squaring complex (imaginary) numbers.

a. -equivalence
b. Complex number
c. -module
d. 2-bridge knot

13. In mathematics, the _____ is a conic section, the intersection of a right circular conical surface and a plane parallel to a generating straight line of that surface. Given a point (the focus) and a line (the directrix) that lie in a plane, the locus of points in that plane that are equidistant to them is a _____.

A particular case arises when the plane is tangent to the conical surface of a circle.

a. -module
b. Parabola
c. 2-bridge knot
d. -equivalence

14. In mathematics, a _____ is a polynomial equation of the second degree. The general form is

$$ax^2 + bx + c = 0$$

The quadratic coefficient a is the coefficient of x^2, the linear coefficient b is the coefficient of x, and c is the constant coefficient, also called the free term or constant term.

Quadratic equations are called quadratic because the variable in the leading term is squared.

a. Rationalisation
b. Cubic function
c. Difference of two squares
d. Quadratic equation

15. In geometry, a _____ is a straight curve. When geometry is used to model the real world, lines are used to represent straight objects with negligible width and height. Lines are an idealisation of such objects and have no width or height at all and are usually considered to be infinitely long.

a. 2-bridge knot
b. -module
c. -equivalence
d. Line

Chapter 4. Exponents and Polynomials

16. In linear algebra, the _____ typically refers to the tensor product of two vectors. The result of applying the _____ to a pair of vectors is a matrix. The name contrasts with the inner product, which takes as input a pair of vectors and produces a scalar.

   a. ADE classification
   b. Abelian P-root group
   c. AKS primality test
   d. Outer product

17. In mathematics, especially in elementary arithmetic, _____ is an arithmetic operation which is the inverse of multiplication.

Specifically, if c times b equals a, written:

$$c \times b = a$$

where b is not zero, then a divided by b equals c, written:

$$\frac{a}{b} = c$$

For instance,

$$\frac{6}{3} = 2$$

since

$$2 \times 3 = 6.$$

In the above expression, a is called the dividend, b the divisor and c the quotient.

   a. -equivalence
   b. 2-bridge knot
   c. -module
   d. Division

18. In mathematics, the _____ and length of a polynomial P with complex coefficients are measures of its 'size'.

For a polynomial P given by

$$P = a_0 + a_1 x + a_2 x^2 + \cdots + a_n x^n,$$

the _____ H(P) is defined to be the maximum of the magnitudes of its coefficients:

$$H(P) = \max_i |a_i|$$

and the length L(P) is similarly defined as the sum of the magnitudes of the coefficients:

$$L(P) = \sum_{i=0}^{n} |a_i|.$$

For a complex polynomial P of degree n, the _____ H(P), length L(P) and Mahler measure M(P) are related by the double inequalities

$$\binom{n}{\lfloor n/2 \rfloor}^{-1} H(P) \le M(P) \le H(P)\sqrt{n+1};$$

$$L(p) \le 2^n M(p) \le 2^n L(p);$$

$$H(p) \le L(p) \le nH(p)$$

where $\binom{n}{\lfloor n/2 \rfloor}$ is the binomial coefficient.

a. Birch and Swinnerton-Dyer conjecture
b. Height
c. Schwartz-Bruhat function
d. Cyclotomic unit

Chapter 5. Factoring and Applications

1. In mathematics, _____(F_n) is the outer automorphism group of a free group on n generators. These groups play an important role in geometric group theory.

   _____(F_n) acts geometrically on a cell complex known as outer space, which can be thought of as the Teichmüller space for a bouquet of circles.

   a. Abelian P-root group
   b. AKS primality test
   c. Out
   d. ADE classification

2. A _____ is a symbol that stands for a value that may vary; the term usually occurs in opposition to constant, which is a symbol for a non-varying value, i.e. completely fixed or fixed in the context of use. The concepts of constants and variables are fundamental to all modern mathematics, science, engineering, and computer programming.

   Much of the basic theory for which we use variables today, such as school geometry and algebra, was developed thousands of years ago, but the use of symbolic formulae and variables is only several hundreds of years old.

   a. -module
   b. 2-bridge knot
   c. -equivalence
   d. Variable

3. In elementary algebra, a _____ is a polynomial consisting of three terms; in other words, a _____ is the sum of three monomials. It can be factored using simple steps.

   In linguistics, a _____ is a fixed expression which is made from three words; e.g. 'lights, camera, action', 'signed, sealed, delivered'.

   a. Hall polynomials
   b. Trinomial
   c. Polynomial Diophantine equation
   d. Finitary operation

Chapter 5. Factoring and Applications

4. In elementary algebra, a _____ is a polynomial with two terms--the sum of two monomials--often bound by parenthesis or brackets when operated upon. It is the simplest kind of polynomial other than monomials.

- The _____ $a^2 - b^2$ can be factored as the product of two other binomials:

    $a^2 - b^2 = (a + b)(a - b.)$

    This is a special case of the more general formula:

    $$a^{n+1} - b^{n+1} = (a - b) \sum_{k=0}^{n} a^k b^{n-k}$$.

- The product of a pair of linear binomials $(ax + b)$ and $(cx + d)$ is:

    $(ax + b)(cx + d) = acx^2 + axd + bcx + bd$.

- A _____ raised to the nth power, represented as

    $(a + b)^n$

    can be expanded by means of the _____ theorem or, equivalently, using Pascal's triangle. Taking a simple example, the perfect square _____ $(p + q)^2$ can be found by squaring the first digit, adding twice the product of the first and second digit and finally adding the square of the second digit, to give $p^2 + 2pq + q^2$.

a. Theory of equations
b. Content
c. Binomial
d. Generalized arithmetic progression

5. A _____ is a three-dimensional solid object bounded by six square faces, facets or sides, with three meeting at each vertex. The _____ can also be called a regular hexahedron and is one of the five Platonic solids. It is a special kind of square prism, of rectangular parallelepiped and of trigonal trapezohedron.
a. Cube
b. -equivalence
c. 2-bridge knot
d. -module

6. In mathematics, _____ or factoring is the decomposition of an object ' href='/wiki/Matrix_(mathematics)'>matrix) into a product of other objects, or factors, which when multiplied together give the original. For example, the number 15 factors into primes as 3 × 5, and the polynomial $x^2 - 4$ factors as $(x - 2)(x + 2.)$ In all cases, a product of simpler objects is obtained.

a. 2-bridge knot
b. -module
c. -equivalence
d. Factorization

7. In mathematics, the word _____ is a term for any well-formed combination of mathematical symbols. For example,

$x^2 + 3x - 4$

is an _____, while

)x) / 0

is not, because the parentheses are not balanced and division by zero is undefined.

Being an _____ is a syntactic concept - the meaning of the variables is irrelevant, but different fields have different notions of validity.â€¢See formal language for how expressions are constructed, and formal semantics for meaning.

a. Orthogonal
b. Unit ring
c. Arity
d. Expression

8. In mathematics, a _____ is a polynomial equation of the second degree. The general form is

$$ax^2 + bx + c = 0$$

The quadratic coefficient a is the coefficient of x^2, the linear coefficient b is the coefficient of x, and c is the constant coefficient, also called the free term or constant term.

Quadratic equations are called quadratic because the variable in the leading term is squared.

a. Quadratic equation
b. Rationalisation
c. Difference of two squares
d. Cubic function

Chapter 5. Factoring and Applications

9. In mathematics, the complex numbers are an extension of the real numbers obtained by adjoining an imaginary unit, denoted i, which satisfies:

$$i^2 = -1.$$

Every _____ can be written in the form a + bi, where a and b are real numbers called the real part and the imaginary part of the _____, respectively.

Complex numbers are a field, and thus have addition, subtraction, multiplication, and division operations. These operations extend the corresponding operations on real numbers, although with a number of additional elegant and useful properties, e.g., negative real numbers can be obtained by squaring complex (imaginary) numbers.

   a. 2-bridge knot
   b. -module
   c. -equivalence
   d. Complex number

10. The _____ are natural numbers including 0 ' href='/wiki/0_(number)'>0, 1, 2, 3, ...) and their negatives (0, −1, −2, −3, ...). They are numbers that can be written without a fractional or decimal component, and fall within the set {...

   a. AKS primality test
   b. ADE classification
   c. Abelian P-root group
   d. Integers

11. A _____ is a triangle in which one angle is a right angle.

The side opposite the right angle is called the hypotenuse (side [BC] in the figure below.) In addition, the sides adjacent to the right angle are called legs or catheti (singular: cathetus.)

   a. 2-bridge knot
   b. -module
   c. -equivalence
   d. Right triangle

12. A _____ is one of the basic shapes of geometry: a polygon with three corners or vertices and three sides or edges which are line segments. A _____ with vertices A, B, and C is denoted ABC.

In Euclidean geometry any three non-collinear points determine a unique _____ and a unique plane (i.e. a two-dimensional Euclidean space.)

a. 2-bridge knot
b. -equivalence
c. Triangle
d. -module

Chapter 6. Rational Expressions and Applications

1. In its simplest meaning in mathematics and logic, an _____ is an action or procedure which produces a new value from one or more input values. There are two common types of operations: unary and binary. Unary operations involve only one value, such as negation and trigonometric functions.
    a. Abelian P-root group
    b. Operation
    c. ADE classification
    d. AKS primality test

2. In mathematics, especially in elementary arithmetic, _____ is an arithmetic operation which is the inverse of multiplication.

Specifically, if c times b equals a, written:

$$c \times b = a$$

where b is not zero, then a divided by b equals c, written:

$$\frac{a}{b} = c$$

For instance,

$$\frac{6}{3} = 2$$

since

$$2 \times 3 = 6.$$

In the above expression, a is called the dividend, b the divisor and c the quotient.

   a. -equivalence
   b. 2-bridge knot
   c. -module
   d. Division

3. In mathematics, the complex numbers are an extension of the real numbers obtained by adjoining an imaginary unit, denoted i, which satisfies:

$$i^2 = -1.$$

Every _____ can be written in the form a + bi, where a and b are real numbers called the real part and the imaginary part of the _____, respectively.

Complex numbers are a field, and thus have addition, subtraction, multiplication, and division operations. These operations extend the corresponding operations on real numbers, although with a number of additional elegant and useful properties, e.g., negative real numbers can be obtained by squaring complex (imaginary) numbers.

   a. -module
   b. -equivalence
   c. 2-bridge knot
   d. Complex number

4. In mathematics, the word _____ is a term for any well-formed combination of mathematical symbols. For example,

   $x^2 + 3x - 4$

is an _____, while

)x) / 0

is not, because the parentheses are not balanced and division by zero is undefined.

Being an _____ is a syntactic concept - the meaning of the variables is irrelevant, but different fields have different notions of validity.â€¢See formal language for how expressions are constructed, and formal semantics for meaning.

   a. Orthogonal
   b. Arity
   c. Unit ring
   d. Expression

5. The _____ of a Lie algebra 𝔤 is a particular ideal of 𝔤.

Let 𝔤 be a Lie algebra. The _____ of 𝔤 is defined as the largest solvable ideal of 𝔤.

a. Radical
b. Cyclically reduced word
c. Class sum
d. Garside element

6. A _____ is a symbol that stands for a value that may vary; the term usually occurs in opposition to constant, which is a symbol for a non-varying value, i.e. completely fixed or fixed in the context of use. The concepts of constants and variables are fundamental to all modern mathematics, science, engineering, and computer programming.

Much of the basic theory for which we use variables today, such as school geometry and algebra, was developed thousands of years ago, but the use of symbolic formulae and variables is only several hundreds of years old.

a. Variable
b. -equivalence
c. 2-bridge knot
d. -module

Chapter 7. Equations of Lines; Functions

1. In mathematics, a (B, N) _____ is a structure on groups of Lie type that allows one to give uniform proofs of many results, instead of giving a large number of case-by-case proofs. Roughly speaking, it shows that all such groups are similar to the general linear group over a field. They were invented by the mathematician Jacques Tits, and are also sometimes known as Tits systems.
    a. Group representations
    b. Group action
    c. Pair
    d. Rank of a group

2. In mathematics, a _____ is a flat surface. Planes can arise as subspaces of some higher dimensional space, as with the walls of a room, or they may enjoy an independent existence in their own right, as in the setting of Euclidean geometry
    a. -equivalence
    b. -module
    c. Similarity
    d. Plane

3. In geometry, a _____ is a straight curve. When geometry is used to model the real world, lines are used to represent straight objects with negligible width and height. Lines are an idealisation of such objects and have no width or height at all and are usually considered to be infinitely long.
    a. Line
    b. 2-bridge knot
    c. -module
    d. -equivalence

4. In mathematics, a _____ is a collection of linear equations involving the same set of variables. For example,

$$3x + 2y - z = 1$$
$$2x - 2y + 4z = -2$$
$$-x + \tfrac{1}{2}y - z = 0$$

is a system of three equations in the three variables x, y, z. A solution to a linear system is an assignment of numbers to the variables such that all the equations are simultaneously satisfied.

a. -equivalence
b. -module
c. Simultaneous equations
d. System of linear equations

5. A _____ is a symbol that stands for a value that may vary; the term usually occurs in opposition to constant, which is a symbol for a non-varying value, i.e. completely fixed or fixed in the context of use. The concepts of constants and variables are fundamental to all modern mathematics, science, engineering, and computer programming.

Much of the basic theory for which we use variables today, such as school geometry and algebra, was developed thousands of years ago, but the use of symbolic formulae and variables is only several hundreds of years old.

a. -module
b. Variable
c. 2-bridge knot
d. -equivalence

6. In mathematics, an _____ is the finite or bounded case of a conic section, the geometric shape that results from cutting a circular conical or cylindrical surface with an oblique plane . It is also the locus of all points of the plane whose distances to two fixed points add to the same constant.

Ellipses also arise as images of a circle or a sphere under parallel projection, and some cases of perspective projection.

a. Ellipse
b. ADE classification
c. AKS primality test
d. Abelian P-root group

7. In mathematics, a _____ is a polynomial equation of the second degree. The general form is

$$ax^2 + bx + c = 0$$

The quadratic coefficient a is the coefficient of x^2, the linear coefficient b is the coefficient of x, and c is the constant coefficient, also called the free term or constant term.

Quadratic equations are called quadratic because the variable in the leading term is squared.

a. Rationalisation
b. Cubic function
c. Difference of two squares
d. Quadratic equation

8. In mathematics, the term _____ is used to describe an algebraic structures which in some sense cannot be divided by a smaller structure of the same type. Put another way, an algebraic structure is _____ if the kernel of every homomorphism is either the whole structure or a single element. Some examples are:

- A group is called a _____ group if it does not contain a non-trivial proper normal subgroup.
- A ring is called a _____ ring if it does not contain a non-trivial two sided ideal.
- A module is called a _____ module if does not contain a non-trivial submodule.
- An algebra is called a _____ algebra if does not contain a non-trivial two sided ideal.

The general pattern is that the structure admits no non-trivial congruence relations.

a. Linear combinations
b. Polarization identity
c. Commutativity
d. Simple

9. In geometry, two lines or planes (or a line and a plane), are considered _____ to each other if they form congruent adjacent angles (an L-shape.) The term may be used as a noun or adjective. Thus, referring to Figure 1, the line AB is the _____ to CD through the point B. Note that by definition, a line is infinitely long, and strictly speaking AB and CD in this example represent line segments of two infinitely long lines.

a. 2-bridge knot
b. Perpendicular
c. -module
d. -equivalence

10. In geometry, a _____ is a part of a line that is bounded by two end points, and contains every point on the line between its end points. Examples of line segments include the sides of a triangle or square. More generally, when the end points are both vertices of a polygon, the _____ is either an edge (of that polygon) if they are adjacent vertices, or otherwise a diagonal.

a. -module
b. Skew lines
c. -equivalence
d. Line segment

11. In mathematics, the complex numbers are an extension of the real numbers obtained by adjoining an imaginary unit, denoted i, which satisfies:

$$i^2 = -1.$$

Every _____ can be written in the form a + bi, where a and b are real numbers called the real part and the imaginary part of the _____, respectively.

Complex numbers are a field, and thus have addition, subtraction, multiplication, and division operations. These operations extend the corresponding operations on real numbers, although with a number of additional elegant and useful properties, e.g., negative real numbers can be obtained by squaring complex (imaginary) numbers.

a. -equivalence
b. -module
c. 2-bridge knot
d. Complex number

12. In mathematics, especially in the area of abstract algebra known as ring theory, a _____ is a ring with 0 ≠ 1 such that ab = 0 implies that either a = 0 or b = 0 (the zero-product property.) That is, it is a nontrivial ring without left or right zero divisors. A commutative _____ is called an integral _____.

a. Coherent ring
b. Domain
c. Partially-ordered ring
d. Subring

13. In mathematics, a _____ is any function which can be written as the ratio of two polynomial functions. _____ of degree 2 : $$y = \frac{x^2 - 3x - 2}{x^2 - 4}$$

In the case of one variable, x, a _____ is a function of the form

$$f(x) = \frac{P(x)}{Q(x)}$$

where P and Q are polynomial function in x and Q is not the zero polynomial. The domain of f is the set of all points x for which the denominator Q(x) is not zero.

a. Rational function
b. -equivalence
c. -module
d. Legendre rational functions

Chapter 8. Systems of Linear Equations

1. An _____ is an equation in a system of simultaneous equations which cannot be derived algebraically from the other equations.
    a. Orthogonalization
    b. Elementary matrix
    c. Independent equation
    d. Eigendecomposition

2. In mathematics, a _____ is a collection of linear equations involving the same set of variables. For example,

$$\begin{aligned} 3x + 2y - z &= 1 \\ 2x - 2y + 4z &= -2 \\ -x + \tfrac{1}{2}y - z &= 0 \end{aligned}$$

is a system of three equations in the three variables x, y, z. A solution to a linear system is an assignment of numbers to the variables such that all the equations are simultaneously satisfied.

    a. -equivalence
    b. Simultaneous equations
    c. System of linear equations
    d. -module

3. A _____ is a symbol that stands for a value that may vary; the term usually occurs in opposition to constant, which is a symbol for a non-varying value, i.e. completely fixed or fixed in the context of use. The concepts of constants and variables are fundamental to all modern mathematics, science, engineering, and computer programming.

Much of the basic theory for which we use variables today, such as school geometry and algebra, was developed thousands of years ago, but the use of symbolic formulae and variables is only several hundreds of years old.

    a. -module
    b. -equivalence
    c. 2-bridge knot
    d. Variable

4. In mathematics, a _____ is a flat surface. Planes can arise as subspaces of some higher dimensional space, as with the walls of a room, or they may enjoy an independent existence in their own right, as in the setting of Euclidean geometry

a. -equivalence
b. -module
c. Similarity
d. Plane

5. In geometry and trigonometry, an _____ is the figure formed by two rays sharing a common endpoint, called the vertex of the _____ . The magnitude of the _____ is the 'amount of rotation' that separates the two rays, and can be measured by considering the length of circular arc swept out when one ray is rotated about the vertex to coincide with the other Where there is no possibility of confusion, the term '_____' is used interchangeably for both the geometric configuration itself and for its angular magnitude (which is simply a numerical quantity.)

a. Abelian P-root group
b. Angle
c. ADE classification
d. AKS primality test

6. A _____ is one of the basic shapes of geometry: a polygon with three corners or vertices and three sides or edges which are line segments. A _____ with vertices A, B, and C is denoted ABC.

In Euclidean geometry any three non-collinear points determine a unique _____ and a unique plane (i.e. a two-dimensional Euclidean space.)

a. 2-bridge knot
b. Triangle
c. -equivalence
d. -module

7. In mathematics, the term _____ is used to describe an algebraic structures which in some sense cannot be divided by a smaller structure of the same type. Put another way, an algebraic structure is _____ if the kernel of every homomorphism is either the whole structure or a single element. Some examples are:

- A group is called a _____ group if it does not contain a non-trivial proper normal subgroup.
- A ring is called a _____ ring if it does not contain a non-trivial two sided ideal.
- A module is called a _____ module if does not contain a non-trivial submodule.
- An algebra is called a _____ algebra if does not contain a non-trivial two sided ideal.

The general pattern is that the structure admits no non-trivial congruence relations.

Chapter 8. Systems of Linear Equations 41

  a. Commutativity
  b. Simple
  c. Polarization identity
  d. Linear combinations

8. In linear algebra, the _____ of a matrix is obtained by changing a matrix in some way.

Given the matrices A and B, where:

$$A = \begin{bmatrix} 1 & 3 & 2 \\ 2 & 0 & 1 \\ 5 & 2 & 2 \end{bmatrix}, \quad B = \begin{bmatrix} 4 \\ 3 \\ 1 \end{bmatrix}$$

Then, the _____ is written as:

$$(A|B) = \begin{bmatrix} 1 & 3 & 2 & 4 \\ 2 & 0 & 1 & 3 \\ 5 & 2 & 2 & 1 \end{bmatrix}$$

This is useful when solving systems of linear equations or the _____ may also be used to find the inverse of a matrix by combining it with the identity matrix.

$$C = \begin{bmatrix} 1 & 3 \\ -5 & 0 \end{bmatrix}$$

Let C be a square 2×2 matrix where

To find the inverse of C we create (C | I) where I is the 2×2 identity matrix.

  a. Unistochastic matrix
  b. Augmented matrix
  c. Euclidean distance matrix
  d. Unitary matrix

9. In mathematics, a _____ is a rectangular array of numbers. This way, matrices can record data that depend on multiple parameters. In particular they are used to keep track of the coefficients of multiple linear equations. Matrices are closely connected to linear transformations, which are higher-dimensional analogs of linear functions, i.e., functions of the form f(x) = c Â· x, where c is a constant. This map corresponds to a _____ with one row and column, with entry c. In addition to a number of elementary, entrywise operations such as _____ addition a key notion is _____ multiplication, which displays a number of features not encountered in numbers; for example, products of matrices depend on the order of the factors, unlike products of real numbers, say, where c Â· d = d Â· c for any two numbers c and d.

a. Heap
b. Commutativity
c. Polynomial expression
d. Matrix

10. In its simplest meaning in mathematics and logic, an _____ is an action or procedure which produces a new value from one or more input values. There are two common types of operations: unary and binary. Unary operations involve only one value, such as negation and trigonometric functions.
   a. ADE classification
   b. Abelian P-root group
   c. AKS primality test
   d. Operation

11. In linear algebra a matrix is in _____ if

   - All nonzero rows are above any rows of all zeroes, and
   - The leading coefficient (also called pivot) of a row is always strictly to the right of the leading coefficient of the row above it.

Some texts add a third condition:

   - The leading coefficient of each nonzero row is one.

A matrix is in reduced _____ if it satisfies the above three conditions, and if, in addition

   - Every leading coefficient is 1 and is the only nonzero entry in its column.

The first non-zero entry in each row is called a pivot.

This matrix is in reduced _____:

$$\begin{bmatrix} 1 & 0 & 0 & 0 & 0 \\ 0 & 1 & 0 & 0 & 0 \\ 0 & 0 & 1 & 0 & 0 \\ 0 & 0 & 0 & 1 & 0 \end{bmatrix}$$

The following matrix is also in _____, but not in reduced row form:

$$\begin{bmatrix} 1 & 9 & 1 & 1 \\ 0 & 1 & 0 & 2 \\ 0 & 0 & 1 & 3 \end{bmatrix}$$

However, this matrix is not in _____, as the leading coefficient of row 3 is not strictly to the right of the leading coefficient of row 2, and the main diagonal is not made up of only ones.

$$\begin{bmatrix} 1 & 2 & 3 & 4 \\ 0 & 3 & 7 & 2 \\ 0 & 2 & 0 & 0 \end{bmatrix}$$

Every non-zero matrix can be reduced to an infinite number of echelon forms (they can all be multiples of each other, for example) via elementary matrix transformations.

a. -module
b. -equivalence
c. 2-bridge knot
d. Row echelon form

Chapter 9. Inequalities and Absolute Value

1. In mathematics, the _____ of two sets A and B is the set that contains all elements of A that also belong to B (or equivalently, all elements of B that also belong to A), but no other elements.

For explanation of the symbols used in this article, refer to the table of mathematical symbols.

The _____ of A and B

The _____ of A and B is written 'A ∩ B'.

   a. ADE classification
   b. AKS primality test
   c. Intersection
   d. Abelian P-root group

2. In its simplest meaning in mathematics and logic, an _____ is an action or procedure which produces a new value from one or more input values. There are two common types of operations: unary and binary. Unary operations involve only one value, such as negation and trigonometric functions.
   a. Abelian P-root group
   b. ADE classification
   c. Operation
   d. AKS primality test

3. In set theory, the term _____ refers to a set operation used in the convergence of set elements to form a resultant set containing the elements of both sets. As a simple example, a _____ of two disjoint sets, which do not have elements in common results in a set containing all elements from both sets. A Venn diagram representing the _____ of sets A and B. If one circle represents A, and the other B, then the red area represents the _____ of A and B. The area where the circles join, also shown in red, is the intersection of the two sets.

If we define two sets which contain unique elements; those of A not occurring in B and vice versa, then the _____ of these sets results in a set which contains all elements of A and B. In terms of notation, we could define this set operation as the following:

   A = {1,2,3,4}
   B = {5,6,7,8}
   $$A \cup B = \{1, 2, 3, 4, 5, 6, 7, 8\}$$

Other more complex operations can be done including the _____, if the set is for example defined by a property rather than a finite or assumed infinite enumeration of elements.

a. AKS primality test
b. Abelian P-root group
c. Union
d. ADE classification

4. In mathematics, the _____ of a real number is its numerical value without regard to its sign. So, for example, 3 is the _____ of both 3 and −3.

The _____ of a number a is denoted by $|a|$.

a. AKS primality test
b. Abelian P-root group
c. ADE classification
d. Absolute value

5. One commonly distinguishes between the _____ and the absolute error. The absolute error is the magnitude of the difference between the exact value and the approximation. The _____ is the absolute error divided by the magnitude of the exact value.
a. Relative error
b. -module
c. 2-bridge knot
d. -equivalence

6. In geometry, a _____ is a straight curve. When geometry is used to model the real world, lines are used to represent straight objects with negligible width and height. Lines are an idealisation of such objects and have no width or height at all and are usually considered to be infinitely long.
a. -module
b. -equivalence
c. 2-bridge knot
d. Line

7. In mathematics, a _____ is a flat surface. Planes can arise as subspaces of some higher dimensional space, as with the walls of a room, or they may enjoy an independent existence in their own right, as in the setting of Euclidean geometry

a. -equivalence
b. -module
c. Similarity
d. Plane

8. A _____ is a symbol that stands for a value that may vary; the term usually occurs in opposition to constant, which is a symbol for a non-varying value, i.e. completely fixed or fixed in the context of use. The concepts of constants and variables are fundamental to all modern mathematics, science, engineering, and computer programming.

Much of the basic theory for which we use variables today, such as school geometry and algebra, was developed thousands of years ago, but the use of symbolic formulae and variables is only several hundreds of years old.

a. -equivalence
b. -module
c. 2-bridge knot
d. Variable

9. In mathematics, _____ is a technique for optimization of a linear objective function, subject to linear equality and linear inequality constraints. Informally, _____ determines the way to achieve the best outcome (such as maximum profit or lowest cost) in a given mathematical model and given some list of requirements represented as linear equations.

More formally, given a polytope (for example, a polygon or a polyhedron), and a real-valued affine function

$$f(x_1, x_2, \ldots, x_n) = c_1 x_1 + c_2 x_2 + \cdots + c_n x_n + d$$

defined on this polytope, a _____ method will find a point in the polytope where this function has the smallest (or largest) value.

a. -equivalence
b. 2-bridge knot
c. Linear programming
d. -module

Chapter 10. Roots, Radicals, and Root Functions

1. The _____ of a Lie algebra $\mathfrak{g}$ is a particular ideal of $\mathfrak{g}$.

   Let $\mathfrak{g}$ be a Lie algebra. The _____ of $\mathfrak{g}$ is defined as the largest solvable ideal of $\mathfrak{g}$.

   a. Garside element
   b. Cyclically reduced word
   c. Radical
   d. Class sum

2. In mathematics, a _____ of a number x is any number which, when repeatedly multiplied by itself, eventually yields x:

   $$r \times r \times \cdots \times r = x.$$

   In terms of exponentiation, r is a _____ of x if

   $$r^n = x$$

   for some positive integer n. For example, 2 is a _____ of 16 since $2^4 = 2 \times 2 \times 2 \times 2 = 16$.

   The number n is called the degree of the _____.

   a. Cubic function
   b. Difference of two squares
   c. Rationalisation
   d. Root

3. In mathematics, a _____ of a number x is a number r such that $r^2 = x$, or, in other words, a number r whose square (the result of multiplying the number by itself) is x.

   Every non-negative real number x has a unique non-negative _____, called the principal _____, which is denoted with a radical symbol as $\sqrt{x}$, or, using exponent notation, as $x^{1/2}$. For example, the principal _____ of 9 is 3, denoted $\sqrt{9} = 3$, because $3^2 = 3 \times 3 = 9$.

   a. 2-bridge knot
   b. -module
   c. -equivalence
   d. Square root

Chapter 10. Roots, Radicals, and Root Functions

4. In elementary algebra, a _____ is a polynomial with two terms--the sum of two monomials--often bound by parenthesis or brackets when operated upon. It is the simplest kind of polynomial other than monomials.

- The _____ $a^2 - b^2$ can be factored as the product of two other binomials:

    $a^2 - b^2 = (a + b)(a - b.)$

    This is a special case of the more general formula:
    $$a^{n+1} - b^{n+1} = (a - b)\sum_{k=0}^{n} a^k b^{n-k}$$.

- The product of a pair of linear binomials $(ax + b)$ and $(cx + d)$ is:

    $(ax + b)(cx + d) = acx^2 + axd + bcx + bd.$

- A _____ raised to the nth power, represented as

    $(a + b)^n$

    can be expanded by means of the _____ theorem or, equivalently, using Pascal's triangle. Taking a simple example, the perfect square _____ $(p + q)^2$ can be found by squaring the :first digit, adding twice the product of the first and second digit and finally adding the square of the second digit, to give $p^2 + 2pq + q^2$.

a. Generalized arithmetic progression
b. Binomial
c. Theory of equations
d. Content

5. A _____ is a three-dimensional solid object bounded by six square faces, facets or sides, with three meeting at each vertex. The _____ can also be called a regular hexahedron and is one of the five Platonic solids. It is a special kind of square prism, of rectangular parallelepiped and of trigonal trapezohedron.
a. -module
b. 2-bridge knot
c. Cube
d. -equivalence

6. In mathematics, a _____ of a number, denoted $\sqrt[3]{x}$ or $x^{1/3}$, is a number a such that $a^3 = x$. All real numbers have exactly one real _____ and a pair of complex conjugate roots, and all nonzero complex numbers have three distinct complex cube roots. For example, the real _____ of 8 is 2, because $2^3 = 8$.

a. -equivalence
b. 2-bridge knot
c. -module
d. Cube root

7. In mathematics, a _____ is any number that can be expressed in the form

$$\frac{a}{b}, a, b \in \mathbb{Z}, b \neq 0$$

which says 'a divided by b, given that a and b are integers and b does not equal zero'. Since the denominator b may be equal to 1, every integer is a _____. The set of all rational numbers is denoted $\mathbb{Q}$ (for quotient.)

a. -equivalence
b. Number system
c. Ratio
d. Rational number

8. In mathematics, specifically group theory, the _____ of a subgroup H in a group G is the e;relative sizee; of H in G. For example, if H has _____ 2 in G, then intuitively e;halfe; of the elements of G lie in H. The _____ of H in G is usually denoted $|G : H|$ or [G : H].

If G and H are finite groups, then the _____ of H in G is simply the quotient of the orders of the two groups:

$$|G : H| = \frac{|G|}{|H|}.$$

By Lagrange's theorem, this number is always a positive integer.

If G and H are infinite, then the _____ of H is G is defined as the number of cosets of H in G.

a. Index
b. Outer automorphism
c. Even permutations
d. Inner automorphism

Chapter 10. Roots, Radicals, and Root Functions

9. In group theory, a branch of mathematics, the term _____ is used in two closely related senses:

    - the _____ of a group is its cardinality, i.e. the number of its elements;
    - the _____, sometimes period, of an element a of a group is the smallest positive integer m such that a^m = e (where e denotes the identity element of the group, and a^m denotes the product of m copies of a.) If no such m exists, we say that a has infinite _____. All elements of finite groups have finite _____.

We denote the _____ of a group G by ord(G) or $|G|$ and the _____ of an element a by ord(a) or $|a|$.

Example. The symmetric group S_3 has the following multiplication table.

This group has six elements, so ord(S_3) = 6.

   a. Index calculus algorithm
   b. Artin group
   c. Outer automorphism group
   d. Order

10. In algebra and computer programming, when a number or expression is both preceded and followed by an operator such as minus or times, a rule is needed to specify which operator should be applied first; this rule is known as a _____, or more informally order of operation. From the earliest use of mathematical notation, multiplication took precedence over addition, whichever side of a number it appeared on. Thus 3 + 4 × 5 = 5 × 4 + 3 = 23.
   a. Precedence rule
   b. Setoid
   c. Formal power series
   d. Planar ternary ring

11. In its simplest meaning in mathematics and logic, an _____ is an action or procedure which produces a new value from one or more input values. There are two common types of operations: unary and binary. Unary operations involve only one value, such as negation and trigonometric functions.
   a. Abelian P-root group
   b. AKS primality test
   c. ADE classification
   d. Operation

12. In mathematics, the word _____ is a term for any well-formed combination of mathematical symbols. For example,

$x^2 + 3x - 4$

is an _____, while

)x) / 0

is not, because the parentheses are not balanced and division by zero is undefined.

Being an _____ is a syntactic concept - the meaning of the variables is irrelevant, but different fields have different notions of validity.â€€See formal language for how expressions are constructed, and formal semantics for meaning.

  a. Unit ring
  b. Expression
  c. Arity
  d. Orthogonal

13. In mathematics, a _____ is a polynomial equation of the second degree. The general form is

$$ax^2 + bx + c = 0$$

The quadratic coefficient a is the coefficient of x^2, the linear coefficient b is the coefficient of x, and c is the constant coefficient, also called the free term or constant term.

Quadratic equations are called quadratic because the variable in the leading term is squared.

  a. Rationalisation
  b. Difference of two squares
  c. Cubic function
  d. Quadratic equation

14. In mathematics, a _____ is a number that can be expressed as an integral of an algebraic function over an algebraic domain. The concept has been promoted by Maxim Kontsevich and Don Zagier.

In elementary mathematics each group of three digits in a number is called a _____

a. -equivalence
b. -module
c. 2-bridge knot
d. Period

15. A _____ is one of the basic shapes of geometry: a polygon with three corners or vertices and three sides or edges which are line segments. A _____ with vertices A, B, and C is denoted ABC.

In Euclidean geometry any three non-collinear points determine a unique _____ and a unique plane (i.e. a two-dimensional Euclidean space.)

a. -equivalence
b. 2-bridge knot
c. -module
d. Triangle

16. The a-_____ of a string, for a a letter, is the number of times that letter occurs in the string. More precisely, let A be a finite set (called the alphabet), $a \in A$ a letter of A, and $c \in A^*$ a string (where A* is the free monoid generated by the elements of A, equivalently the set of strings, including the empty string, whose letters are from A.) Then the a-_____ of c, denoted by $wt_a(c)$, is the number of times the generator a occurs in the unique expression for c as a product (concatenation) of letters in A.
a. Weight
b. Biordered set
c. Trace monoid
d. Presentation of a monoid

17. In algebra, a _____ of an element in a quadratic extension field of a field K is its image under the unique non-identity automorphism of the extended field that fixes K. If the extension is generated by a square root of an element r of K, then the _____ of $a + b\sqrt{r}$ is $a - b\sqrt{r}$ for $a, b \in K$, and in particular in the case of the field C of complex numbers as an extension of the field R of real numbers (where r = − 1), the complex _____ of a + bi is a − bi.

Forming the sum or product of any element of the extension field with its _____ always gives an element of K. This can be used to rewrite a quotient of numbers in the extended field so that the denominator lies in K, by multiplying numerator and denominator by the _____ of the denominator. This process is called rationalization of the denominator, in particular if K is the field Q of rational numbers.

a. Field arithmetic
b. K-theory
c. Digital root
d. Conjugate

18. A _____ is a triangle in which one angle is a right angle.

The side opposite the right angle is called the hypotenuse (side [BC] in the figure below.) In addition, the sides adjacent to the right angle are called legs or catheti (singular: cathetus.)

a. Right triangle
b. 2-bridge knot
c. -equivalence
d. -module

19. _____ is the mathematical process of putting things together. The plus sign '+' means that numbers are added together. For example, in the picture on the right, there are 3 + 2 apples--meaning three apples and two other apples--which is the same as five apples, since 3 + 2 = 5.

a. Addition
b. AKS primality test
c. ADE classification
d. Abelian P-root group

20. _____ is one of the four basic arithmetic operations; it is the inverse of addition, meaning that if we start with any number and add any number and then subtract the same number we added, we return to the number we started with. _____ is denoted by a minus sign in infix notation.

The traditional names for the parts of the formula

　　c − b = a

are minuend (c) − subtrahend (b) = difference (a.)

a. -equivalence
b. Subtraction
c. 2-bridge knot
d. -module

Chapter 10. Roots, Radicals, and Root Functions

21. A _____ is an expression which compares quantities relative to each other. The most common examples involve two quantities, but in theory any number of quantities can be compared. In mathematical terms, they are represented by separating each quantity with a colon, for example the _____ 2:3, which is read as the _____ 'two to three'.
   a. Number system
   b. Rational number
   c. -equivalence
   d. Ratio

22. In mathematics, especially in elementary arithmetic, _____ is an arithmetic operation which is the inverse of multiplication.

Specifically, if c times b equals a, written:

$$c \times b = a$$

where b is not zero, then a divided by b equals c, written:

$$\frac{a}{b} = c$$

For instance,

$$\frac{6}{3} = 2$$

since

$$2 \times 3 = 6.$$

In the above expression, a is called the dividend, b the divisor and c the quotient.

   a. -equivalence
   b. -module
   c. 2-bridge knot
   d. Division

23. In mathematics, the complex numbers are an extension of the real numbers obtained by adjoining an imaginary unit, denoted i, which satisfies:

$i^2 = -1.$

Every _____ can be written in the form a + bi, where a and b are real numbers called the real part and the imaginary part of the _____, respectively.

Complex numbers are a field, and thus have addition, subtraction, multiplication, and division operations. These operations extend the corresponding operations on real numbers, although with a number of additional elegant and useful properties, e.g., negative real numbers can be obtained by squaring complex (imaginary) numbers.

a. -module
b. 2-bridge knot
c. -equivalence
d. Complex number

24. In mathematics, an _____ represents a solution, such as that to an equation, that emerges from the process of solving the problem but is not a valid solution to the original problem. A missing solution is a solution that was a valid solution to the original problem, but disappeared during the process of solving the problem. Both are frequently the consequence of performing operations that are not invertible for some or all values of the variables, which disturbs the chain of logical implications in the proof.
    a. Equating the coefficients
    b. Unitary method
    c. Unary operation
    d. Extraneous solution

25. In mathematics, an _____ is a complex number whose squared value is a real number less than or equal to zero. The imaginary unit, denoted by i or j, is an example of an _____. If y is a real number, then iÂ·y is an _____, because:

$$(i \cdot y)^2 = i^2 \cdot y^2 = -y^2 \leq 0.$$

Imaginary numbers were defined in 1572 by Rafael Bombelli.

a. ADE classification
b. AKS primality test
c. Abelian P-root group
d. Imaginary number

Chapter 10. Roots, Radicals, and Root Functions

26. In mathematics, the _____ of a real number is its numerical value without regard to its sign. So, for example, 3 is the _____ of both 3 and −3.

The _____ of a number a is denoted by $|a|$.

   a. Abelian P-root group
   b. Absolute value
   c. AKS primality test
   d. ADE classification

27. In mathematics, the (formal) _____ of a complex vector space V is the complex vector space $\overline{V}$ consisting of all formal complex conjugates of elements of V. That is, $\overline{V}$ is a vector space whose elements are in one-to-one correspondence with the elements of V:

$$\overline{V} = \{\overline{v} \mid v \in V\},$$

with the following rules for addition and scalar multiplication:

$$\overline{v} + \overline{w} = \overline{v + w} \quad \text{and} \quad \alpha \overline{v} = \overline{\overline{\alpha} v}.$$

Here v and w are vectors in V, α is a complex number, and $\overline{\alpha}$ denotes the _____ of α.

In the case where V is a linear subspace of $\mathbb{C}^n$, the formal _____ $\overline{V}$ is naturally isomorphic to the actual _____ subspace of V in $\mathbb{C}^n$.

   a. Binomial inverse theorem
   b. Polynomial basis
   c. Conjugate transpose
   d. Complex conjugate

Chapter 11. Quadratic Equations, Inequalities, and Functions

1. In elementary algebra, _____ is a technique for converting a quadratic polynomial of the form

$$ax^2 + bx + c$$

to the form

$$a(\cdots\cdots)^2 + \text{constant}.$$

The expression inside the parenthesis is of the form x − constant. Thus one converts ax² + bx + c to

$$a(x - h)^2 + k$$

and one must find h and k.

_____ is used in

- solving quadratic equations,
- graphing quadratic functions,
- evaluating integrals in calculus,
- finding Laplace transforms.

In mathematics, _____ is considered a basic algebraic operation, and is often applied without remark in any computation involving quadratic polynomials.

There is a simple formula in elementary algebra for computing the square of a binomial:

$$(x + p)^2 = x^2 + 2px + p^2.$$

For example:

$$(x + 3)^2 = x^2 + 6x + 9 \qquad (p = 3)$$
$$(x - 5)^2 = x^2 - 10x + 25 \qquad (p = -5).$$

In any perfect square, the number p is always half the coefficient of x, and then the constant term is equal to p².

   a. Completing the square
   b. Nested radical
   c. Content
   d. Reduct

2. In mathematics, a _____ is a polynomial equation of the second degree. The general form is

Chapter 11. Quadratic Equations, Inequalities, and Functions

$$ax^2 + bx + c = 0$$

The quadratic coefficient a is the coefficient of x^2, the linear coefficient b is the coefficient of x, and c is the constant coefficient, also called the free term or constant term.

Quadratic equations are called quadratic because the variable in the leading term is squared.

a. Cubic function
b. Quadratic equation
c. Rationalisation
d. Difference of two squares

3. In abstract algebra, a _____ is a function on an algebra which generalizes certain features of the derivative operator. Specifically, given an algebra A over a ring or a field F, an F-_____ is an F-linear map D: A → A that satisfies Leibniz's law:

D(ab) = (Da)b + a(Db.)

More generally, an F-linear map D of A into an A-module M, satisfying the Leibniz law is also called a _____. The collection of all F-derivations of A to itself is denoted by Der$_F$(A.)

a. Derivation
b. Transcendental function
c. Differential algebras
d. Pincherle derivative

4. In algebra, the _____ of a polynomial with real or complex coefficients is a certain expression in the coefficients of the polynomial which is a symmetric polynomial in the coefficients and gives information on the nature of the roots; in particular, it is equal to zero if and only if the polynomial has a multiple root (i.e. a root with multiplicity greater than one) in the complex numbers. For example, the _____ of the quadratic polynomial

$$ax^2 + bx + c \text{ is } b^2 - 4ac.$$

The _____ of the cubic polynomial

$$ax^3 + bx^2 + cx + d \text{ is } b^2c^2 - 4ac^3 - 4b^3d - 27a^2d^2 + 18abcd.$$

Chapter 11. Quadratic Equations, Inequalities, and Functions

 a. Kazhdan-Lusztig polynomials
 b. Minimal polynomial
 c. Polynomial remainder theorem
 d. Discriminant

5. A _____ is a symbol that stands for a value that may vary; the term usually occurs in opposition to constant, which is a symbol for a non-varying value, i.e. completely fixed or fixed in the context of use. The concepts of constants and variables are fundamental to all modern mathematics, science, engineering, and computer programming.

Much of the basic theory for which we use variables today, such as school geometry and algebra, was developed thousands of years ago, but the use of symbolic formulae and variables is only several hundreds of years old.

 a. -equivalence
 b. 2-bridge knot
 c. -module
 d. Variable

6. In mathematics, the _____ is a conic section, the intersection of a right circular conical surface and a plane parallel to a generating straight line of that surface. Given a point (the focus) and a line (the directrix) that lie in a plane, the locus of points in that plane that are equidistant to them is a _____.

A particular case arises when the plane is tangent to the conical surface of a circle.

 a. 2-bridge knot
 b. Parabola
 c. -equivalence
 d. -module

7. A _____, in mathematics, is a polynomial function of the form f(x) = ax² + bx + c = 0, where $a \neq 0$. The graph of a _____ is a parabola whose major axis is parallel to the y-axis.

The expression ax² + bx + c in the definition of a _____ is a polynomial of degree 2 or second order, or a 2nd degree polynomial, because the highest exponent of x is 2.

Chapter 11. Quadratic Equations, Inequalities, and Functions

a. Factor theorem
b. Dickson polynomials
c. Vandermonde polynomial
d. Quadratic function

8. In elementary algebra, a _____ is a polynomial with two terms--the sum of two monomials--often bound by parenthesis or brackets when operated upon. It is the simplest kind of polynomial other than monomials.

- The _____ $a^2 - b^2$ can be factored as the product of two other binomials:

    $a^2 - b^2 = (a + b)(a - b.)$

    This is a special case of the more general formula:

    $$a^{n+1} - b^{n+1} = (a - b) \sum_{k=0}^{n} a^k b^{n-k}$$

- The product of a pair of linear binomials (ax + b) and (cx + d) is:

    $(ax + b)(cx + d) = acx^2 + axd + bcx + bd.$

- A _____ raised to the nth power, represented as

    $(a + b)^n$

    can be expanded by means of the _____ theorem or, equivalently, using Pascal's triangle. Taking a simple example, the perfect square _____ $(p + q)^2$ can be found by squaring the first digit, adding twice the product of the first and second digit and finally adding the square of the second digit, to give $p^2 + 2pq + q^2$.

a. Content
b. Generalized arithmetic progression
c. Binomial
d. Theory of equations

9. In mathematics, the term _____ is used to describe an algebraic structures which in some sense cannot be divided by a smaller structure of the same type. Put another way, an algebraic structure is _____ if the kernel of every homomorphism is either the whole structure or a single element. Some examples are:

- A group is called a _____ group if it does not contain a non-trivial proper normal subgroup.
- A ring is called a _____ ring if it does not contain a non-trivial two sided ideal.
- A module is called a _____ module if does not contain a non-trivial submodule.
- An algebra is called a _____ algebra if does not contain a non-trivial two sided ideal.

The general pattern is that the structure admits no non-trivial congruence relations.

Chapter 11. Quadratic Equations, Inequalities, and Functions

a. Commutativity
b. Linear combinations
c. Polarization identity
d. Simple

10. In a totally ordered set all elements are mutually comparable, so such a set can have at most one minimal element and at most one maximal element. Then, due to mutual comparability, the minimal element will also be the least element and the maximal element will also be the greatest element. Thus in a totally ordered set we can simply use the terms _____ and maximum.

a. Minimum
b. 2-bridge knot
c. -equivalence
d. -module

11. In geometry, the foci, pronounced , are a pair of special points used in describing conic sections. The four types of conic sections are the circle, parabola, ellipse, and hyperbola.

The _____ has two equivalent defining properties; and they always fall on the major axis of symmetry of the conic.

a. Derivation of the cartesian form for an ellipse
b. Focus
c. Conic section
d. Dandelin spheres

12. In mathematics, an _____ is a statement about the relative size or order of two objects, or about whether they are the same or not

- The notation a < b means that a is less than b.
- The notation a > b means that a is greater than b.
- The notation a ≠ b means that a is not equal to b, but does not say that one is bigger than the other or even that they can be compared in size.

In all these cases, a is not equal to b, hence, '_____'.

These relations are known as strict _____

- The notation a ≤ b means that a is less than or equal to b (or, equivalently, not greater than b);
- The notation a ≥ b means that a is greater than or equal to b (or, equivalently, not smaller than b);

Chapter 11. Quadratic Equations, Inequalities, and Functions

An additional use of the notation is to show that one quantity is much greater than another, normally by several orders of magnitude.

- The notation a ≪ b means that a is much less than b.
- The notation a ≫ b means that a is much greater than b.

If the sense of the _____ is the same for all values of the variables for which its members are defined, then the _____ is called an 'absolute' or 'unconditional' _____. If the sense of an _____ holds only for certain values of the variables involved, but is reversed or destroyed for other values of the variables, it is called a conditional _____.

One can apply the same algebraic operations to inequalities as one would apply for solving equalities. For example, to find x for the _____ 10x > 20 one would divide 20 by 10 to obtain x > 2.

a. AKS primality test
b. ADE classification
c. Abelian P-root group
d. Inequality

13. In mathematics, a _____ in a topological space X is a continuous map f from the unit interval I = [0,1] to X

    f : I → X.

The initial point of the _____ is f(0) and the terminal point is f(1.) One often speaks of a '_____ from x to y' where x and y are the initial and terminal points of the _____.

a. Genus
b. Simplicial complex
c. Suspension
d. Path

Chapter 12. Inverse, Exponential, and Logarithmic Functions

1. In geometry, a _____ is a straight curve. When geometry is used to model the real world, lines are used to represent straight objects with negligible width and height. Lines are an idealisation of such objects and have no width or height at all and are usually considered to be infinitely long.
    a. 2-bridge knot
    b. -equivalence
    c. -module
    d. Line

2. Any formula written in terms of logarithms may be said to be in _____.

In contexts including complex manifolds and algebraic geometry, a logarithmic differential form is a 1-form that, locally at least, can be written

$$\frac{df}{f}$$

for some meromorphic function (resp. rational function) f.

    a. Meromorphic function
    b. Bispectrum
    c. Hankel contour
    d. Logarithmic form

3. In geometry, two lines or planes (or a line and a plane), are considered _____ to each other if they form congruent adjacent angles (an L-shape.) The term may be used as a noun or adjective. Thus, referring to Figure 1, the line AB is the _____ to CD through the point B. Note that by definition, a line is infinitely long, and strictly speaking AB and CD in this example represent line segments of two infinitely long lines.
    a. Perpendicular
    b. -module
    c. 2-bridge knot
    d. -equivalence

4. In mathematics, the term _____ is used to describe an algebraic structures which in some sense cannot be divided by a smaller structure of the same type. Put another way, an algebraic structure is _____ if the kernel of every homomorphism is either the whole structure or a single element. Some examples are:

- A group is called a _____ group if it does not contain a non-trivial proper normal subgroup.
- A ring is called a _____ ring if it does not contain a non-trivial two sided ideal.
- A module is called a _____ module if does not contain a non-trivial submodule.
- An algebra is called a _____ algebra if does not contain a non-trivial two sided ideal.

The general pattern is that the structure admits no non-trivial congruence relations.

a. Simple
b. Polarization identity
c. Commutativity
d. Linear combinations

Chapter 13. Nonlinear Functions, Conic Sections, and Nonlinear Systems

1. In mathematics, a _____ is a curve obtained by intersecting a cone (more precisely, a circular conical surface) with a plane. A _____ is therefore a restriction of a quadric surface to the plane. The conic sections were named and studied as long ago as 200 BC, when Apollonius of Perga undertook a systematic study of their properties.
    a. Conic section
    b. Derivation of the cartesian form for an ellipse
    c. Dandelin spheres
    d. Matrix representation of conic sections

2. In the mathematical field of topology, a _____ of a fiber bundle, π: E → B, over a topological space, B, is a continuous map, s : B → E, such that π(s(x))=x for all x in B.

    A _____ is a certain generalization of the notion of the graph of a function. The graph of a function g : X → Y can be identified with a function taking its values in the Cartesian product E = X×Y of X and Y:

    $$s(x) = (x, g(x)) \in E, \quad s : X \to E.$$

    A _____ is an abstract characterization of what it means to be a graph.

    a. -equivalence
    b. Fiber bundle
    c. -module
    d. Section

3. In mathematics, the _____ of a real number is its numerical value without regard to its sign. So, for example, 3 is the _____ of both 3 and −3.

    The _____ of a number a is denoted by $|a|$.

    a. Absolute value
    b. ADE classification
    c. Abelian P-root group
    d. AKS primality test

4. In mathematics, a _____ of a number x is a number r such that r^2 = x, or, in other words, a number r whose square (the result of multiplying the number by itself) is x.

    Every non-negative real number x has a unique non-negative _____, called the principal _____, which is denoted with a radical symbol as $\sqrt{x}$, or, using exponent notation, as $x^{1/2}$. For example, the principal _____ of 9 is 3, denoted $\sqrt{9} = 3$, because 3^2 = 3 × 3 = 9.

a. Square root
b. -module
c. -equivalence
d. 2-bridge knot

5. In mathematics, a _____ is a polynomial equation of the second degree. The general form is

$$ax^2 + bx + c = 0$$

The quadratic coefficient a is the coefficient of x^2, the linear coefficient b is the coefficient of x, and c is the constant coefficient, also called the free term or constant term.

Quadratic equations are called quadratic because the variable in the leading term is squared.

a. Difference of two squares
b. Quadratic equation
c. Rationalisation
d. Cubic function

6. In mathematics, a _____ of a number x is any number which, when repeatedly multiplied by itself, eventually yields x:

$$r \times r \times \cdots \times r = x.$$

In terms of exponentiation, r is a _____ of x if

$$r^n = x$$

for some positive integer n. For example, 2 is a _____ of 16 since $2^4 = 2 \times 2 \times 2 \times 2 = 16$.

The number n is called the degree of the _____.

a. Root
b. Cubic function
c. Rationalisation
d. Difference of two squares

7. The _____ are natural numbers including 0 ' href='/wiki/0_(number)'>0, 1, 2, 3, ...) and their negatives (0, −1, −2, −3, ...). They are numbers that can be written without a fractional or decimal component, and fall within the set {...

Chapter 13. Nonlinear Functions, Conic Sections, and Nonlinear Systems

a. AKS primality test
b. Integers
c. ADE classification
d. Abelian P-root group

8. The term _____ or centre is used in various contexts in abstract algebra to denote the set of all those elements that commute with all other elements. More specifically:

- The _____ of a group G consists of all those elements x in G such that xg = gx for all g in G. This is a normal subgroup of G.
- The _____ of a ring R is the subset of R consisting of all those elements x of R such that xr = rx for all r in R. The _____ is a commutative subring of R, so R is an algebra over its _____.
- The _____ of an algebra A consists of all those elements x of A such that xa = ax for all a in A. See also: central simple algebra.
- The _____ of a Lie algebra L consists of all those elements x in L such that [x,a] = 0 for all a in L. This is an ideal of the Lie algebra L.
- The _____ of a monoidal category C consists of pairs (A,u) where A is an object of C, and $u : A \otimes - \to - \otimes A$ a natural isomorphism satisfying certain axioms.

a. Center
b. Ring theory
c. Left alternative
d. Self-adjoint

9. In mathematics, an _____ is the finite or bounded case of a conic section, the geometric shape that results from cutting a circular conical or cylindrical surface with an oblique plane . It is also the locus of all points of the plane whose distances to two fixed points add to the same constant.

Ellipses also arise as images of a circle or a sphere under parallel projection, and some cases of perspective projection.

a. Abelian P-root group
b. ADE classification
c. AKS primality test
d. Ellipse

10. In mathematics, a _____ in a topological space X is a continuous map f from the unit interval I = [0,1] to X

Chapter 13. Nonlinear Functions, Conic Sections, and Nonlinear Systems

$f : I \to X$.

The initial point of the _____ is f(0) and the terminal point is f(1.) One often speaks of a '_____ from x to y' where x and y are the initial and terminal points of the _____.

a. Simplicial complex
b. Genus
c. Suspension
d. Path

Chapter 14. Sequences and Series

1. In algebra, a commutative ring R is said to be _____ if any of the following equivalent conditions holds:

   1. The localization $R_\mathfrak{m}$ of R at $\mathfrak{m}$ is a valuation ring for every maximal ideal $\mathfrak{m}$ of R.
   2. For all ideals $\mathfrak{a}, \mathfrak{b}$, and $\mathfrak{c}$,

   $$\mathfrak{a} \cap (\mathfrak{b} + \mathfrak{c}) = (\mathfrak{a} \cap \mathfrak{b}) + (\mathfrak{a} \cap \mathfrak{c})$$

- For all ideals $\mathfrak{a}, \mathfrak{b}$, and $\mathfrak{c}$,

$$\mathfrak{a} + (\mathfrak{b} \cap \mathfrak{c}) = (\mathfrak{a} + \mathfrak{b}) \cap (\mathfrak{a} + \mathfrak{c})$$

An _____ domain is called a Prüfer domain.

   a. Exchange matrix
   b. Ordered vector space
   c. Inverse eigenvalues theorem
   d. Arithmetical

2. In mathematics, specifically group theory, the _____ of a subgroup H in a group G is the e;relative sizee; of H in G. For example, if H has _____ 2 in G, then intuitively e;halfe; of the elements of G lie in H. The _____ of H in G is usually denoted $|G:H|$ or $[G:H]$.

If G and H are finite groups, then the _____ of H in G is simply the quotient of the orders of the two groups:

$$|G:H| = \frac{|G|}{|H|}.$$

By Lagrange's theorem, this number is always a positive integer.

If G and H are infinite, then the _____ of H is G is defined as the number of cosets of H in G.

   a. Index
   b. Outer automorphism
   c. Inner automorphism
   d. Even permutations

3. The _____ of a Lie algebra $\mathfrak{g}$ is a particular ideal of $\mathfrak{g}$.

Let $\mathfrak{g}$ be a Lie algebra. The _____ of $\mathfrak{g}$ is defined as the largest solvable ideal of $\mathfrak{g}$.

a. Garside element
b. Cyclically reduced word
c. Class sum
d. Radical

4. A _____ is an expression which compares quantities relative to each other. The most common examples involve two quantities, but in theory any number of quantities can be compared. In mathematical terms, they are represented by separating each quantity with a colon, for example the _____ 2:3, which is read as the _____ 'two to three'.
a. Rational number
b. Ratio
c. -equivalence
d. Number system

5. In mathematics, a _____ is a number that can be expressed as an integral of an algebraic function over an algebraic domain. The concept has been promoted by Maxim Kontsevich and Don Zagier.

In elementary mathematics each group of three digits in a number is called a _____

a. -module
b. Period
c. 2-bridge knot
d. -equivalence

Chapter 14. Sequences and Series

6. In elementary algebra, a _____ is a polynomial with two terms--the sum of two monomials--often bound by parenthesis or brackets when operated upon. It is the simplest kind of polynomial other than monomials.

- The _____ a² - b² can be factored as the product of two other binomials:

    a² - b² = (a + b)(a - b.)

    This is a special case of the more general formula:
    $$a^{n+1} - b^{n+1} = (a-b)\sum_{k=0}^{n} a^k b^{n-k}$$

- The product of a pair of linear binomials (ax + b) and (cx + d) is:

    (ax + b)(cx + d) = acx² + axd + bcx + bd.

- A _____ raised to the nth power, represented as

    (a + b)^n

    can be expanded by means of the _____ theorem or, equivalently, using Pascal's triangle. Taking a simple example, the perfect square _____ (p + q)² can be found by squaring the :first digit, adding twice the product of the first and second digit and finally adding the square of the second digit, to give p² + 2pq + q².

a. Binomial
b. Content
c. Theory of equations
d. Generalized arithmetic progression

7. In mathematics, the _____ is an important formula giving the expansion of powers of sums. Its simplest version states that

$$(x+y)^n = \sum_{k=0}^{n} \binom{n}{k} x^{n-k} y^k \qquad (1)$$

for any real or complex numbers x and y, and any non-negative integer n. The binomial coefficient appearing in (1) may be defined in terms of the factorial function n!:

$$\binom{n}{k} = \frac{n!}{k!\,(n-k)!}.$$

For example, here are the cases where 2 ≤ n ≤ 5:

$$(x+y)^2 = x^2 + 2xy + y^2$$
$$(x+y)^3 = x^3 + 3x^2y + 3xy^2 + y^3$$
$$(x+y)^4 = x^4 + 4x^3y + 6x^2y^2 + 4xy^3 + y^4$$
$$(x+y)^5 = x^5 + 5x^4y + 10x^3y^2 + 10x^2y^3 + 5xy^4 + y^5.$$

Formula (1) is valid more generally for any elements x and y of a semiring as long as xy = yx.

  a. 2-bridge knot
  b. Binomial theorem
  c. -equivalence
  d. -module

8. A _____ is one of the basic shapes of geometry: a polygon with three corners or vertices and three sides or edges which are line segments. A _____ with vertices A, B, and C is denoted ABC.

In Euclidean geometry any three non-collinear points determine a unique _____ and a unique plane (i.e. a two-dimensional Euclidean space.)

  a. -module
  b. Triangle
  c. 2-bridge knot
  d. -equivalence

9. In mathematics, an _____ of a product of sums expresses it as a sum of products by using the fact that multiplication distributes over addition. Expansions of polynomials are obtained by multiplying together their factors, which results in a sum of terms with variables raised to different degrees.

To multiply two factors, each term of the first factor must be multiplied by each term of the other factor.

  a. Equipotential surfaces
  b. Analytic subgroup
  c. Ordered vector space
  d. Expansion

Chapter 14. Sequences and Series

10. In its simplest meaning in mathematics and logic, an _____ is an action or procedure which produces a new value from one or more input values. There are two common types of operations: unary and binary. Unary operations involve only one value, such as negation and trigonometric functions.
    a. Abelian P-root group
    b. Operation
    c. ADE classification
    d. AKS primality test

11. In mathematics, a _____ of a number x is a number r such that r^2 = x, or, in other words, a number r whose square (the result of multiplying the number by itself) is x.

    Every non-negative real number x has a unique non-negative _____, called the principal _____, which is denoted with a radical symbol as $\sqrt{x}$, or, using exponent notation, as $x^{1/2}$. For example, the principal _____ of 9 is 3, denoted $\sqrt{9} = 3$, because 3^2 = 3 × 3 = 9.

    a. -equivalence
    b. -module
    c. Square root
    d. 2-bridge knot

12. In mathematics, a _____ of a number x is any number which, when repeatedly multiplied by itself, eventually yields x:

    $$r \times r \times \cdots \times r = x.$$

    In terms of exponentiation, r is a _____ of x if

    $$r^n = x$$

    for some positive integer n. For example, 2 is a _____ of 16 since 2^4 = 2 × 2 × 2 × 2 = 16.

    The number n is called the degree of the _____.

    a. Rationalisation
    b. Difference of two squares
    c. Root
    d. Cubic function

Chapter 14. Sequences and Series

13. _____ is the mathematical process of putting things together. The plus sign '+' means that numbers are added together. For example, in the picture on the right, there are 3 + 2 apples--meaning three apples and two other apples--which is the same as five apples, since 3 + 2 = 5.
    a. AKS primality test
    b. Abelian P-root group
    c. ADE classification
    d. Addition

14. _____ is one of the four basic arithmetic operations; it is the inverse of addition, meaning that if we start with any number and add any number and then subtract the same number we added, we return to the number we started with. _____ is denoted by a minus sign in infix notation.

The traditional names for the parts of the formula

   c − b = a

are minuend (c) − subtrahend (b) = difference (a.)

    a. -module
    b. 2-bridge knot
    c. -equivalence
    d. Subtraction

15. In mathematics, the _____ of a real number is its numerical value without regard to its sign. So, for example, 3 is the _____ of both 3 and −3.

The _____ of a number a is denoted by $|a|$.

    a. Absolute value
    b. Abelian P-root group
    c. ADE classification
    d. AKS primality test

16. In mathematics, the complex numbers are an extension of the real numbers obtained by adjoining an imaginary unit, denoted i, which satisfies:

$$i^2 = -1.$$

Chapter 14. Sequences and Series

Every _____ can be written in the form a + bi, where a and b are real numbers called the real part and the imaginary part of the _____, respectively.

Complex numbers are a field, and thus have addition, subtraction, multiplication, and division operations. These operations extend the corresponding operations on real numbers, although with a number of additional elegant and useful properties, e.g., negative real numbers can be obtained by squaring complex (imaginary) numbers.

   a. -equivalence
   b. Complex number
   c. 2-bridge knot
   d. -module

17. In mathematics, especially in elementary arithmetic, _____ is an arithmetic operation which is the inverse of multiplication.

Specifically, if c times b equals a, written:

$$c \times b = a$$

where b is not zero, then a divided by b equals c, written:

$$\frac{a}{b} = c$$

For instance,

$$\frac{6}{3} = 2$$

since

$$2 \times 3 = 6.$$

In the above expression, a is called the dividend, b the divisor and c the quotient.

   a. 2-bridge knot
   b. -module
   c. Division
   d. -equivalence

Chapter 14. Sequences and Series

18. In mathematics, and more specifically set theory, the _____ is the unique set having no (zero) members. Some axiomatic set theories assure that the _____ exists by including an axiom of _____; in other theories, its existence can be deduced. Many possible properties of sets are trivially true for the _____.
    a. Abelian P-root group
    b. ADE classification
    c. AKS primality test
    d. Empty set

19. In mathematics, a _____ is a rectangular array of numbers. This way, matrices can record data that depend on multiple parameters. In particular they are used to keep track of the coefficients of multiple linear equations. Matrices are closely connected to linear transformations, which are higher-dimensional analogs of linear functions, i.e., functions of the form f(x) = c Â· x, where c is a constant. This map corresponds to a _____ with one row and column, with entry c. In addition to a number of elementary, entrywise operations such as _____ addition a key notion is _____ multiplication, which displays a number of features not encountered in numbers; for example, products of matrices depend on the order of the factors, unlike products of real numbers, say, where c Â· d = d Â· c for any two numbers c and d.
    a. Heap
    b. Commutativity
    c. Polynomial expression
    d. Matrix

20. In discrete mathematics and predominantly in set theory, a _____ is a concept used in comparisons of sets to refer to the unique values of one set in relation to another. The terms 'absolute' and 'relative' _____ refer to more specific applications of the concept, with universal complements referring to elements unique to the universal set and the latter referring to the unique elements of one set in relation to another. In this image, the universal set is represented by the border of the image, and the set A as a disc.
    a. -module
    b. -equivalence
    c. Pointed set
    d. Complement

21. In mathematics, the _____ of two sets A and B is the set that contains all elements of A that also belong to B (or equivalently, all elements of B that also belong to A), but no other elements.

For explanation of the symbols used in this article, refer to the table of mathematical symbols.

The _____ of A and B

The _____ of A and B is written 'A ∩ B'.

a. ADE classification
b. Abelian P-root group
c. Intersection
d. AKS primality test

22. In set theory, the term _____ refers to a set operation used in the convergence of set elements to form a resultant set containing the elements of both sets. As a simple example, a _____ of two disjoint sets, which do not have elements in common results in a set containing all elements from both sets. A Venn diagram representing the _____ of sets A and B. If one circle represents A, and the other B, then the red area represents the _____ of A and B. The area where the circles join, also shown in red, is the intersection of the two sets.

If we define two sets which contain unique elements; those of A not occurring in B and vice versa, then the _____ of these sets results in a set which contains all elements of A and B. In terms of notation, we could define this set operation as the following:

A = {1,2,3,4}
B = {5,6,7,8}
$$A \cup B = \{1, 2, 3, 4, 5, 6, 7, 8\}$$

Other more complex operations can be done including the _____, if the set is for example defined by a property rather than a finite or assumed infinite enumeration of elements.

a. AKS primality test
b. Union
c. ADE classification
d. Abelian P-root group

23. In probability theory and statistics, a _____ is described as the number separating the higher half of a sample, a population from the lower half. The _____ of a finite list of numbers can be found by arranging all the observations from lowest value to highest value and picking the middle one. If there is an even number of observations, the _____ is not unique, so one often takes the mean of the two middle values.
a. 2-bridge knot
b. -equivalence
c. Median
d. -module

24. In abstract algebra, the _____ of a module is a measure of the module's 'size'. It is defined as the _____ of the longest ascending chain of submodules and is a generalization of the concept of dimension for vector spaces. The modules with finite _____ share many important properties with finite-dimensional vector spaces.

Chapter 14. Sequences and Series

   a. Finitely generated module
   b. Morita equivalence
   c. Supermodule
   d. Length

25. In mathematics, a _____ in a (unital) ring R is an invertible element of R, i.e. an element u such that there is a v in R with

   uv = vu = 1_R, where 1_R is the multiplicative identity element.

That is, u is an invertible element of the multiplicative monoid of R. If $0 \neq 1$ in the ring, then 0 is not a _____.

Unfortunately, the term _____ is also used to refer to the identity element 1_R of the ring, in expressions like ring with a _____ or _____ ring, and also e.g. '_____' matrix.

   a. Ore condition
   b. Ore extension
   c. Ascending chain condition on principal ideals
   d. Unit

26. In geometry, a _____ is a straight curve. When geometry is used to model the real world, lines are used to represent straight objects with negligible width and height. Lines are an idealisation of such objects and have no width or height at all and are usually considered to be infinitely long.
   a. -equivalence
   b. 2-bridge knot
   c. Line
   d. -module

27. The a-_____ of a string, for a a letter, is the number of times that letter occurs in the string. More precisely, let A be a finite set (called the alphabet), $a \in A$ a letter of A, and $c \in A^*$ a string (where A* is the free monoid generated by the elements of A, equivalently the set of strings, including the empty string, whose letters are from A.) Then the a-_____ of c, denoted by $wt_a(c)$, is the number of times the generator a occurs in the unique expression for c as a product (concatenation) of letters in A.

Chapter 14. Sequences and Series

   a. Weight
   b. Biordered set
   c. Presentation of a monoid
   d. Trace monoid

28. In algebra, a _____ is a function depending on n that associates a scalar, det(A), to an n×n square matrix A. The fundamental geometric meaning of a _____ is a scale factor for measure when A is regarded as a linear transformation. Determinants are important both in calculus, where they enter the substitution rule for several variables, and in multilinear algebra.

For a fixed nonnegative integer n, there is a unique _____ function for the n×n matrices over any commutative ring R. In particular, this function exists when R is the field of real or complex numbers.

   a. Functional determinant
   b. Leibniz formula
   c. Pfaffian
   d. Determinant

29. In linear algebra, a _____ of a matrix A is the determinant of some smaller square matrix, cut down from A by removing one or more of its rows or columns. Minors obtained by removing just one row and one column from square matrices (first minors) are required for calculating matrix cofactors, which in turn are useful for computing both the determinant and inverse of square matrices.
   a. Supergroup
   b. Rng
   c. Purification
   d. Minor

30. In abstract algebra, a _____ is a function on an algebra which generalizes certain features of the derivative operator. Specifically, given an algebra A over a ring or a field F, an F-_____ is an F-linear map D: A → A that satisfies Leibniz's law:

   D(ab) = (Da)b + a(Db.)

More generally, an F-linear map D of A into an A-module M, satisfying the Leibniz law is also called a _____. The collection of all F-derivations of A to itself is denoted by $Der_F(A.)$

a. Pincherle derivative
b. Transcendental function
c. Differential algebras
d. Derivation

ANSWER KEY

Chapter 1
1. d   2. d   3. d   4. d   5. d   6. a   7. b   8. d   9. d   10. a
11. b   12. a   13. c   14. d   15. a   16. a   17. d   18. c   19. c   20. c
21. c   22. b   23. d   24. a

Chapter 2
1. d   2. b   3. d   4. a   5. c   6. d   7. a   8. d   9. c   10. a
11. c   12. d   13. d   14. d   15. b   16. d

Chapter 3
1. d   2. b   3. c   4. d   5. c   6. d   7. b   8. d   9. d

Chapter 4
1. d   2. d   3. c   4. a   5. d   6. d   7. d   8. d   9. d   10. d
11. d   12. b   13. b   14. d   15. d   16. d   17. d   18. b

Chapter 5
1. c   2. d   3. b   4. c   5. a   6. d   7. d   8. a   9. d   10. d
11. d   12. c

Chapter 6
1. b   2. d   3. d   4. d   5. a   6. a

Chapter 7
1. c   2. d   3. a   4. d   5. b   6. a   7. d   8. d   9. b   10. d
11. d   12. b   13. a

Chapter 8
1. c   2. c   3. d   4. d   5. b   6. b   7. b   8. b   9. d   10. d
11. d

Chapter 9
1. c   2. c   3. c   4. d   5. a   6. d   7. d   8. d   9. c

Chapter 10
1. c   2. d   3. d   4. b   5. c   6. d   7. d   8. a   9. d   10. a
11. d   12. b   13. d   14. d   15. d   16. a   17. d   18. a   19. a   20. b
21. d   22. d   23. d   24. d   25. d   26. b   27. d

Chapter 11
1. a   2. b   3. a   4. d   5. d   6. b   7. d   8. c   9. d   10. a
11. b   12. d   13. d

Chapter 12
1. d   2. d   3. a   4. a

Chapter 13

| 1. a | 2. d | 3. a | 4. a | 5. b | 6. a | 7. b | 8. a | 9. d | 10. d |

Chapter 14

1. d	2. a	3. d	4. b	5. b	6. a	7. b	8. b	9. d	10. b
11. c	12. c	13. d	14. d	15. a	16. b	17. c	18. d	19. d	20. d
21. c	22. b	23. c	24. d	25. d	26. c	27. a	28. d	29. d	30. d

www.ingramcontent.com/pod-product-compliance
Lightning Source LLC
Chambersburg PA
CBHW081848230426
43669CB00018B/2870